FREE

AMID LIFE'S DIFFICULT MOMENTS

*HOW THE CHRISTIAN LIFE CAN
RELEASE A CAPTIVE HEART*

THE SECOND STEP

DONALD E. JONES, PHD

J & A Book Publishers
www.jabookpublishers.com

ISBN-13: 978-1-946368-28-7

FIRST BOOKS IN THE SERIES
(Read one of these books first based on the issues you face)

CALM AMID LIFE'S FINAL MOMENTS
HOW THE GOSPEL CAN BRING CALM TO A TROUBLED HEART THE FIRST STEP

COMFORT AMID LIFE'S PAIN-FILLED MOMENTS
HOW THE GOSPEL CAN BRING RELIEF TO A TORMENTED HEART THE FIRST STEP

CONTENT AMID LIFE'S EMPTY MOMENTS
HOW THE GOSPEL CAN FULFILL A BARREN HEART THE FIRST STEP

COURAGE AMID LIFE'S TRAGIC MOMENTS
HOW THE GOSPEL CAN BRING STRENGTH TO A DESPERATE HEART THE FIRST STEP

FAITH AMID LIFE'S WRONG TURNS
HOW THE GOSPEL CAN BRING MERCY TO A REGRETFUL HEART THE FIRST STEP

GRACE AMID LIFE'S WAYWARD MOMENTS
HOW THE GOSPEL CAN BRING RELIEF TO A GUILTY HEART THE FIRST STEP

HOPE AMID LIFE'S DEPRESSING MOMENTS
HOW THE GOSPEL CAN BRING HOPE TO A DESPAIRING HEART THE FIRST STEP

LOVE AMID LIFE'S BROKEN RELATIONSHIPS
HOW THE GOSPEL CAN MEND A SHATTERED HEART THE FIRST STEP

PEACE AMID LIFE'S ANXIOUS MOMENTS
HOW THE GOSPEL CAN BRING PEACE TO A WORRIED HEART THE FIRST STEP

PURPOSE AMID LIFE'S AIMLESS MOMENTS
HOW THE GOSPEL CAN BRING PURPOSE TO A WANDERING HEART THE FIRST STEP

TRUST AMID LIFE'S FINANCIAL CRISES
HOW THE GOSPEL CAN BRING CONFIDENCE TO AN UNCERTAIN HEART THE FIRST STEP

SECOND BOOK IN THE SERIES
(Read this book second if the issues continue)

FREE AMID LIFE'S DIFFICULT MOMENTS
HOW THE CHRISTIAN LIFE CAN RELEASE A CAPTIVE HEART THE SECOND STEP

THIRD BOOK IN THE SERIES
(Read this book third if the issues continue)

JOY AMID LIFE'S CHALLENGING MOMENTS
HOW THE WORD OF GOD CAN RELIEVE A BURDENED HEART THE THIRD STEP

CONTENTS

ACKNOWLEDGMENTS

I want to thank my wonderful and gracious wife Carol who has supported me in this ministry with sacrifice, enthusiasm, encouragement, and accountability. Most of all, she has been a constant blessing because of her willingness to listen. I was always sharing with her the truths God had been teaching me as I studied His word and wrote this book. It consumed many hours. Thank you, Carol and I deeply love you.

I want to thank my son Gregory R. Jones for volunteering to be the primary editor of this important book. Without his time and effort in painstakingly and meticulously going over every word and every sentence checking and rechecking the sentence structure and grammar, I would not have been able to complete it. Thank you for your ministry to me.

I want to thank my other children, Krista, Matt, and Kara for their love for Christ and His Word and their willingness to live for Him. I love you all.

Introduction

Life had thrown many difficulties at Onesimus, the slave of a man named Philemon. He had mostly been his servant in bondage his entire life and had finally mustered up the courage to escape. After stealing some expensive items from his master's home to sustain him during his journey, he ran for his life. He traveled to the capital city of the Roman Empire to blend into the crowd and hopefully avoid arrest. He knew that he was Philemon's property, and if he were caught, his master could punish him in a multitude of ways. There could be beatings, chains, branding on the forehead "runaway", or even death.

For now, he would have to live on the streets and beg or depend on some type of criminal activity just to stay alive. At best, he would live a quiet but meager life, and he would always be looking over his shoulder. Most likely, his new life as a runaway was filled with emptiness, fear, torment, physical pain, desperation, despair, stress, anxiety, regret, brokenness, guilt, and uncertainty. He must have initially wandered without aim through the streets of Rome.

It was in this difficult situation that this runaway slave met the apostle Paul and found lasting freedom in Jesus Christ. This would have burst forth into the calm, peace, joy, faith, comfort, hope, love, grace, courage, purpose, and trust we seek. How could this have happened? Paul was in chains living in the capital city of Rome awaiting trial before Caesar for the false charges of blasphemy against the Jews and sedition against the empire. Since he was not a criminal, he was allowed to have guests. Through God's sovereignty, he met Onesimus and brought him to Jesus Christ. Though Onesimus was a runaway slave, he was a capable man. Paul needed his abilities and gifts to minister to the people.

Since Paul had also brought his master Philemon to the Lord, he took some liberty as an apostle and spiritual father to both these men and used Onesimus for ministry as long as he could. Now, it was time for the slave to return to his master Philemon and face the many consequences for his crimes. Paul was not going to allow Philemon to make a judgment toward his fellow brother in Christ without a letter directly from him. When Onesimus returned, the letter was with him. This was Paul's letter to Philemon.

Paul's letter recommended that Philemon reconcile with Onesimus and welcome him as a brother in Christ rather than as a fugitive slave who deserved severe punishment. Among other reasons, Paul explained that the Lord God had allowed his slave to run away in order to save the man. Philemon now had Onesimus back as a beloved brother in the flesh and in the Lord Jesus Christ. Out of his own pocket, the apostle would himself pay for any money lost. Philemon must have welcomed Onesimus back with open arms because the new brother in Christ became a valuable member of the church at Colossae.

Any emptiness, fear, torment, pain, desperation, despair, stress, anxiety, brokenness, regret, guilt, and uncertainty he may have had as a runaway, would have faded first as he found salvation in Christ. Now, Onesimus could trust the Lord Jesus in all things as a new child of God. Secondly, any of the emptiness, fear, torment, physical pain, desperation, despair, stress, anxiety, brokenness, regret, guilt, or financial uncertainty that this new saint may still have felt would continue to dissipate as Paul and Philemon ministered to him in his new Christian life. His newfound faith in Christ Jesus would have brought an assurance of eternal life. In and of itself, this may have been enough. He could now trust in Jesus no matter what came his way. Then, his growth in his faith would continue the process.

This book describes the next steps in our spiritual journey toward dealing with some of the most difficult problems that life can bring. The "First Step" books of this series, which preceded this second book, dealt with the essential issues that people face and described exactly how receiving Jesus Christ as Savior and Lord could bring relief. As we read one of them, we found that salvation in the Lord could bring relief from the burden we were facing. This is not due to the fact that the Lord Jesus came to solve our temporal problems and meet our felt needs but they would certainly be a result.

Instead, as we saw in the first book of this series, the Lord Jesus came to build a kingdom which would stretch into all eternity. God, the Father, gave His Son a kingdom of people who would glorify Him forever. As Christians did this, the Son and His kingdom would also glorify the Father. This would be done in the power of the Holy Spirit. All would enjoy a deep and abiding fellowship together. To accomplish this, we would have to be redeemed from the penalty of our sins through the death of Jesus on the cross. Once saved, we would begin the task of bringing others into the kingdom and preparing ourselves to meet Christ when He returns.

Through our salvation, much of the stress and strain of the difficulties we face are eliminated as we redefine our lives as now "in Him" and as the Spirit begins to indwell us. Yet, due to our fallen humanity, we might still be struggling with some of these old issues while encountering new ones. Much of this agony can be tackled by embracing all that the Christian life can offer. After one receives Jesus Christ as Savior and Lord, one must pursue after all that the Christian life entails. In Philippians 2:12-13, Paul commands, "So then, my beloved, even as you have always obeyed, not only in my presence, but now...in my absence work out your own salvation with fear and trembling. For it is God who works in you both to will and to work, for his good pleasure."

This church in Philippi had allowed life to overwhelm them and had lost much of their real joy. Though the apostle provides many solutions, the key had to do with aligning themselves with God's purpose for calling them in the first place. They needed to begin "working out all aspects of their salvation" and God would do the same alongside them. Salvation is not the end; it is the beginning and there is much life to be lived in Him. As we embrace it fully and work out its principles, the Lord God will also work in us. These are not "good works" that save but the many actions which must be taken as we participate in the building of the kingdom of God on earth until He returns.

As God's people become more and more involved in this incredible supernatural adventure, they will discover more and more freedom from the chains that bind them. They will find themselves caught up in the many powerful pursuits of the kingdom of God. Our Christian lives must be centered on Him and living in His Kingdom and looking forward to our redemption in heaven. The result of changing the focus of our lives with its many needs to Christ and His desires is to find His contentment, His fulfillment, His comfort, His calm, His courage, His faith, His grace, His hope, His love, His peace, His purpose, and also His trust. This second book discusses how to live strong Christian lives that will result in greater relief from whatever is troubling us.

One Last Thought:

As a Christian Pastoral Counselor addressing very serious life problems in this second book, I realize the possibility that someone might be reading this and contemplating suicide. If this is the case, please do not hesitate to call 911 or go to the nearest emergency room or hospital immediately. **(And take this book with you!)**

Chapter 1

Concentrate on Spiritual Growth

To release our captive hearts and finally find the freedom we seek amid life's difficult moments, we must concentrate on spiritual growth in our daily lives. We cannot deny the absolute importance of growing in all areas, but our growth in Christ becomes our primary focus and the other areas of our earthly life are secondary. To grow spiritually is to be transformed into the likeness of Jesus Christ. Our Father, God, desires for His children to think, speak, and act more and more like His Son in their lives on this earth. Being a Christian or a follower of Christ does not mean becoming the best of who we are, it means becoming the best of who He is in us. In Galatians 2:20, Paul describes this truth, "I have been crucified with Christ, and it is no longer I that live, but Christ living in me. That life which I now live in the flesh, I live by faith in the Son of God, who loved me, and gave himself up for me." For this does not simply entail following Christ alone but becoming like Him in every way we are able. It is growing into the very image of Christ.

How does this affect the difficulties that we are facing and were discussed in the "First Step" books? Once we receive Christ, our eternity is settled, the Spirit comes to indwell us, and we become "new people." This change can settle much, if not all, of the issues we face and the feelings that follow. Yet, this may not completely solve the problem because we can still think, feel, speak, and act like our "old selves" which could be the source of whatever the challenges we still have. These might include a fear of death, a general emptiness, a tormented, pain-filled body, a regret for past sinful actions, a desperation facing tragedy, a guilt for past mistakes, a deep

5

despair, a broken heart, a sense of anxiety, a lack of purpose, or financial uncertainty. Since the Lord was able to overcome these difficulties, as we grow to be like Him, we will too.

The Lord Jesus experienced every kind of issue, problem, difficulty, and temptation we are now facing and was able to overcome them all. In Philippians 2:7-8, Paul explains the absolutely full humanity of Jesus when he left His heavenly abode and became a man. He writes, "But emptied himself, taking the form of a servant, being made in the likeness of men. And being found in human form [appearance], he humbled himself, becoming obedient to death, yes, the death of the cross." The Lord took on the likeness and appearance of a man. These words refer to our human bodies, needs, desires, and customs. He was a first century Jewish man, except that He did not have a "sin principle" residing in His body. He was completely pure of heart and mind. He was like the Adam before he sinned.

As a result, Jesus experienced our human infirmities and temptations. In Hebrews 4:15, it says, "For we don't have a high priest [Jesus] who can't be touched with the feeling of our infirmities, but one who has been in all points tempted like we are, yet without sin." In Hebrews 5:8, the author describes His suffering in these words, "Though he was a Son, yet learned obedience by the things which he suffered." The Lord learned to follow God as He suffered for us. In fact, between the Garden of Gethsemane where He cried, "Father, take this cup from me" and the cross where He moaned, "My God, My God, why have you forsaken me," I would say He experienced the emptiness, fear, desperation, torment, pain, despair, brokenness, anxiety, regret and guilt (for our sins, not His), aimlessness, and uncertainty that we may feel. As a result, as we grow in His image, we will be able to overcome these similar kinds of issues. This process of sanctification is powerful and utterly supernatural.

How was Jesus able to handle all that He faced? First, He had God's perspective on all that He did. He saw everything in light of God's sovereignty, power, will, and His purpose on earth. As a result, He did not entangle Himself in the affairs of life because He had a supernatural purpose and a divine perspective. In John 5:30, the Lord Jesus states, "I can of myself do nothing. As I hear, I judge, and my judgment is righteous; because I don't seek my own will, but the will of my Father who sent me." Here, the Lord explains that He knew His purpose and focused on that. We can also know our purpose and focus on this. What is that purpose? It is to grow in Christ by practicing the principles from the Bible presented in this book. These are the basic purposes of our lives. In 2 Timothy 2:4, Paul warned Timothy with these words, "No soldier on duty entangles himself in the affairs of life, that he may please him who enrolled him as a soldier." The chains that we bear chains can easily come from our entanglement of the affairs of the world and its many concerns. We need to not allow them to entangle us. We cannot buckle under their bondage.

Second, Jesus relied on the His Spirit. At His Baptism, the Spirit came upon Him and led Him throughout His entire ministry (Matthew 3:16; 4:1). When we became Christians, the Holy Spirit came upon us. In 1 Corinthians 3:16, Paul asks, "Don't you know that you are a temple of God, and that God's Spirit lives in you?" Since the Spirit indwells us, we will walk in him. In Romans 8:1, Paul states, "There is therefore now no condemnation to those who are in Christ Jesus, who don't walk according to the flesh, but according to the Spirit." Then, when we walk according to the Spirit, He will fill us with His supernatural fruits: love, joy, peace, patience, kindness, goodness, faith, and gentleness, Also, He gives us the much-needed self-control (Galatians 5:22-23). These loosen chains and bring release from our bondage. In becoming more like Christ by following His principles is real freedom from our captivity.

Third, as we grow in Jesus Christ, we will learn to set our minds on the things above where the lord's mind also was. In Colossians 3:2, the apostle Paul commands, "Set your mind on the things that are above, not on the things that are on the earth." We can do this by practicing the principles of growth. In Romans 8:5-6, Paul discusses their results, "For those who live according to the flesh set their minds on the things of the flesh, but those who live according to the Spirit, the things of the Spirit. For the mind of the flesh is death, but the mind of the Spirit is life and peace." Notice that it leads to life and peace. These words refer to a full Christian life with peace in our hearts. Will this not unshackle us?

So, what does spiritual growth entail? In Ephesians 4:12-13, Paul describes a key purpose of the pastor's work in our lives as teaching, preaching, and shepherding. He writes, "For the perfecting [maturing] of the saints, to the work of serving, to the building up of the body of Christ; until we all [individually and together] attain to the unity of the faith, and of the knowledge of the Son of God, to a full-grown man, to the measure of the stature of the fullness of Christ." Without endeavoring to unpack every part of this passage, we need to simply note that the goal of every believer is to measure up to the "stature of the fullness of Christ." This would be like a brother standing next to his older brother attempting to grow into his image. He would be checking his height, weight, and build. We are standing next to Christ and growing into his spiritual image checking our spiritual character, attitudes, and lifestyle. Just as the younger brother desired to think, speak, and even act like his older brother so we do the same regarding Christ.

What does this really mean? If Christ was dependent on God, we learn to be dependent on God. If Christ was patient, we learn to be patient. If Christ obeyed God's commands, we learn to obey God's commands. This growth process into the image of Jesus Christ is mentioned in numerous places in the New Testament. Let us look at just a few.

In Colossians 2:19, to describe our spiritual growth, Paul compares the members of the church, the Body of Christ, to the physical members of a body. In this passage he declares, "And not holding firmly to the Head, from whom all the body, being supplied and knit together through the joints and ligaments, grows with God's growth." Like a human organism with a physical body that has all of its parts joined together so does the church. Then as a physical body grows in its individual parts causing the growth in the whole body so does the church. We are all to grow more and more like Him individually in our thoughts, words, and deeds. When we gather together and touch one another's lives, this causes us to think, speak, and act like Christ together.

In 1 Corinthians 3:6-7, the apostle uses a different analogy to speak of our growth both individually and together. Paul compares us to a plant that needs to be planted and watered so God can cause growth. He writes, "I planted. Apollos watered. But God gave the increase. So then neither he who plants is anything, nor he who waters, but God who gives the increase." Here again, each individual part of the plant will grow and cause the whole plant to grow.

In the book of Ephesians, Paul speaks of the church as a building which is growing into a holy temple. In verse 21, Paul describes it this way, "In whom the whole building, fitted together, grows into a holy temple in the Lord." Once again, we see the word "grow." Spiritual growth is the focus of our lives both individually and corporately (as we meet together locally). The Lord Jesus is not an add-on to a life; He becomes the very center of the life we desire to live. In Galatians 2:20, Paul describes it, "I have been crucified with Christ, and it is no longer I that live, but Christ living in me.

That life which I now live in the flesh, I live by faith in the Son of God, who loved me, and gave himself up for me."

How can all of these things truly occur in our very busy lives? The answer is found in realizing that we now have new lives in Christ. We are not adding Christ to a busy life; instead, we are entering a process of changing our lives to center around the kingdom of God. In 2 Corinthians 5:17, Paul describes us, "Therefore if anyone is in Christ, he is a new creation. The old things have passed away. Behold, all things have become new." The Greek word translated "new" in English means "brand new of a different kind" as opposed to "new of the same kind." We now have a truly brand-new life; it is utterly different, incredibly spiritual, and indelibly sacred and holy. We have awakened spiritually.

The journey or adventure I mentioned earlier involves the process of growing in this new life. It is a process of slowly and meticulously putting off the old life and putting on the new life. It is a beautiful lifetime process. In Ephesians 4:22-24, Paul explains this, "That you put away, as concerning your former way of life, the old man, that grows corrupt after the lusts of deceit; and that you be renewed in the spirit of your mind and put on the new [of a different kind] man, who in the likeness of God has been created in righteousness and holiness of truth."

This process Paul is addressing will take time and effort but produces as a result a "brand new of a different kind" contentment, calm, comfort, courage, faith, grace, hope, love, peace, purpose, and trust. The old manner of life only brings their opposites which have been plaguing us all along. We could shed the emptiness, fear, torment, pain, desperation, regret, guilt, despair, brokenness, anxiety, aimlessness, or uncertainty. The new manner of life in Jesus Christ produces a supernatural aspect that cannot be found without Him.

As we proceed through the different elements of spiritual growth in the chapters ahead, we should keep the following considerations in mind. By doing this, we will find the calm, peace, joy, faith, comfort, hope, love, grace, trust, courage, and purpose, we need. Again, the purpose of our lives is spiritual growth in Christ and these things I just mentioned are the fruits and benefits. We must keep in mind that Jesus is the center of our world, not ourselves.

First, we should give ourselves time to grow and time to overcome the issues we face as we grow. The Lord Jesus was patient as the disciples grew into their full understanding of who He truly was and then began to think, speak, and act like Him. A classic example involves the disciples in a frightening moment at sea. In Matthew 8:23-27, the apostle describes it in these words, "When he [Jesus] got into a boat, his disciples followed him. Behold, a violent storm came up on the sea, so much that the boat was covered with the waves, but he was asleep. They came to him, and woke [Jesus] him up, saying, "Save us, Lord! We are dying!" He said to them, "Why are you fearful, O you of little faith?" Then he got up, rebuked the wind and the sea, and there was a great calm. The men marveled, saying, "What kind of man is this, that even the wind and the sea obey him?"

In this example the disciples knew who He was but did not understand the full extent of His power. As a result, they could not react in the same way as He did to the storm with calm and a sense of peace and security. To grow into the image of Christ, we must first know everything about Him in order to imitate Him. This means we must understand His thoughts and ways in a deeper way, and this takes time.

After this, we see a similar incident demonstrating they still did not understand. In Matthew 14:21-27, the Lord had just fed the crowd with a few loaves and fish. Matthew, an eyewitness, now records what happened next, "Those who ate [the food] were about five thousand men, besides women and children. Immediately, Jesus made the disciples get into the boat, and to go ahead of him to the other side, while he sent the multitudes away. After he had sent the multitudes away, he [Jesus] went up into the mountain by himself to pray. When evening had come, he was there alone. But the boat was now in the middle of the sea, distressed by...waves, for the wind was contrary. In the fourth watch of the night, Jesus came to them, walking on the sea. When the disciples [not just Peter alone] saw him walking on the sea, they were troubled, saying, 'It's a ghost!' and they [the disciples] cried out for fear. But immediately Jesus spoke to them, saying 'Cheer up! It is I! Don't be afraid.'" If they didn't understand His power, it was displayed now! Then, Peter speaks.

In verses 28-30, Matthew continues, "Peter answered him and said, 'Lord, if it is you, command me to come to you on the waters.' He said, 'Come!' Peter stepped down from the boat and walked on the waters to come to Jesus. But when he [Peter] saw that the wind was strong, he was afraid, and beginning to sink, he cried out, saying, 'Lord, save me!' Immediately Jesus stretched out his hand, took hold of him, and said to him, 'You of little faith, why did you doubt?' When they got up into the boat, the wind ceased. Those who were in the boat came and worshiped him, saying, 'You are truly the Son of God!'" Though all the disciples were present at this incredible event, Peter's response is the one that is focused upon. This is significant.

Peter still cannot comprehend the extent of Christ's power and stumbles in his faith. The disciple sees the violent winds and begins to sink. Desperately, he reaches out his hand and Jesus takes it. Why? The Lord knows that we must grow in our understanding of Him so we may grow in our imitation of Him. Growing in Christ will take time and involve much stumbling and making mistakes. The Lord was patient, and we need to be patient with ourselves. What does this mean? The elements of spiritual growth will allow us to mature in our understanding of Christ. Then, we will be able to live like Him, but this might require much effort. We may have much difficulty following them so being persistent, patient, and consistent in our pursuit is really important.

As we are giving ourselves time, we should keep moving forward in your spiritual growth. In the New Testament, the Christian life is compared to a "walk." When we walk, we normally don't walk backward but only forward. We may stumble back, often at first, but we must keep moving forward. In Colossians 2:6, the apostle Paul describes it this way, "As therefore you received Christ Jesus, the Lord, walk in him." We are to live our entire lives one step at a time in His presence. In Romans 6:4, he says, "We were buried therefore with him through baptism to death, that just as Christ was raised from the dead through the glory of the Father, so we also might walk in newness of life." This "walking" is a new way of living our lives. It has nothing to do with our old way of which we are accustomed.

In Romans 8:1, Paul adds this truth, "There is therefore now no condemnation to those who are in Christ Jesus, who don't walk according to the flesh [our sinful old ways], but according to the Spirit." A sin principle resides in our bodies can affect our beliefs, feelings, and attitudes. These in turn can influence our thoughts, words and actions. This occurs when we walk by the flesh. When we walk in the Spirit by following the principles we are about to discuss in the chapters ahead, we will display the thoughts, words, and actions of Christ. In Galatians 5:16, Paul explains, "But I say, walk by the Spirit, and you won't fulfill the lust of the flesh." When we stumble, we should confess our sins and keep moving forward. In 1 John 1:9, John, the apostle, provides the pattern of repenting and confessing as we walk and stumble, "If we confess our sins, he is faithful and righteous to forgive us the sins, and to cleanse us from all unrighteousness."

Peter stumbled many times but kept moving forward. He attempted to defend the Lord Jesus at His arrest against a mob (John 18:10) and was bold enough to follow the Lord to the very courtyard of the high priest. Then he stumbled by becoming fearful and denying that he even knew the Lord Jesus when challenged (John 18:17-27). Afterward, Peter wept bitterly. Then, Peter repented and confessed that terrible sin. Later, Jesus restored Peter to his position of leadership among the disciples (John 21:14-18).

At Pentecost and beyond, Peter spoke the gospel boldly to the people (Acts 2:14; 3:12). His boldness in preaching was matched by his boldness in facing persecution for it. After this, the apostles were arrested and told not to preach Christ ever again. Peter with John courageously told those leaders that they would obey God and continue proclaiming the gospel (Acts 4:1-31). Later, Peter would stop eating with the Christian Gentiles in Antioch because he was fearful and wanted to appease the Jews. As a result, Paul was compelled to openly confront him for his hypocrisy. Of course, Peter repented (Galatians 2:11-15). It would be ludicrous to think that the chief apostle of Jesus Christ did not repent when he was legitimately confronted. Peter was constantly moving forward even after much stumbling; he never gave up. He preached and preached. He wrote two letters to the churches and was eventually martyred for his faith.

The Christians life is a lifelong journey toward maturity in Christ and the sooner we realize this the better. We are not expected to become instant mature Christians. In 1 John 2:12-14, the apostle John describes three stages of maturity in Christ. In this passage, John appeals to believers at these three levels to heed his remarks about loving the brethren and practicing righteousness. He writes, "I write to you, little children, because your sins are forgiven you for his name's sake. I write to you, fathers, because you know him who is from the beginning. I write to you, young men, because you have overcome the evil one. I write to you, little [spiritual] children, because you know the Father. I have written to you, [spiritual] fathers, because you know him who is from the beginning. I have written to you, [spiritual] young men, because you are strong, and the word of God remains in you, and you have overcome the evil one."

Though Paul uses two different words in the Greek for children, he is speaking of the same level of maturity. Those who are children in Christ know that God is their father, and their sins are forgiven. They rejoice that they all are in the family of God and that they have full forgiveness. They walk like toddlers and know that when they make mistakes their "daddy" will forgive them. These are believers who speak of God's love and grace, know a few Scriptures here and there, and know that they are going to heaven.

Young men in the true faith are spiritually strong in their walk, know the Holy Scriptures well, and are battling and overcoming the Devil on a regular basis. When young men live their Christian lives, it is based not on love, grace, and forgiveness but on the deep and abiding truths of the Word, and they pursue after righteousness. Spiritual fathers deeply know and understand the God behind the love, grace, and forgiveness. They know the Holy Scriptures, have fought the battles many days, and are beginning to see the God behind it all. The apostle John repeats the phrase "because you know him who is from the beginning." Who is the Him? It is none other than the triune God. The Godhead has been there from the beginning of time and from the beginning of the earth. We can grow to know Him better.

15

In John 1:1-3, the apostle adds, "In the beginning was the Word, and the Word was with God, and the Word was God. The same was in the beginning with God. All things were made through him. Without him was not anything made that has been made." Spiritual fathers have taken the words spoken by Him, lived a life devoted to Him, and now begin to know and understand the depth and majesty of who God truly is. They cry out as Paul does in 1 Timothy 1:17, "Now to the King eternal, immortal, invisible, to God who alone is wise, be honor and glory forever and ever. Amen."

Our goal in this life is to progress through these powerful Christian stages to become like Him because we know Him. We have so read and lived the Holy Scriptures that we now understand the thoughts, words, and actions of God so they become our thoughts, words, and actions. This will lead to the release our captive hearts. Then, we will finally find the freedom we are seeking amid life's difficult moments. As we turn our attention to spiritual growth in our daily lives, we will grow more and more into His image. As we do this, we will experience more and more the sense of calm, peace, joy, faith, comfort, hope, love, grace, courage, purpose, and trust we desire.

Chapter 2

Walk With Spiritual Intention

For us to spiritually grow in Christ, we must view our time differently. In our old lives, our time was our own and we did what we wanted with it; now our time is His and we should dedicate it to Him. To accomplish this, we have to change from unintentional living to intentional. In Ephesians 5:15-16, Paul writes, "Therefore be careful how you walk, not as unwise men but as wise, making the most of your time, because the days are evil." Most of the challenges we face, which continue to plague us, could be conquered through living the Christian life in a consistent and vibrant way. If we desire freedom from the chains of our emptiness, fear of death, torment, pain, desperation, regret, guilt, brokenness, despair, anxiety, aimlessness, or uncertainty, we must fully pursue the one goal of building up kingdom of God through serious intentional living.

Wrapping ourselves up the prison of our many woes will not alleviate any of the feelings we have. Instead, we must dive into the "living water" of the Holy Spirit. This is not an emotional experience, but it is an action plan. After water baptism, the next action we must take to settle our issues is to dedicate time to our new Lord Jesus. We must remember that the purpose of this kingdom was to be a love gift from the Father to the Son. The Son desired to give that gift back to the Father and the Holy Spirit empowered it all. Our lives are to be lived for the glory of God so we must get control of them. We should not be pursuing after our desires only.

We can do this by walking with spiritual intention. In the passage just mentioned, this is done first by "careful" living.

The Greek word used here indicates "a long and careful look to perceive what is happening." We should pay close attention to what we are actually doing with our time. Once this occurs, we should manage our time more wisely. The saints cannot just "hang out" or involve themselves in useless endeavors. This "wisdom" doesn't refer to our own personal wisdom or the wisdom of others; but instead, it denotes the wisdom of God which is found in the Bible. In Proverbs 2:6, Solomon wrote, "For Yahweh gives wisdom. Out of His mouth comes knowledge and understanding." Where do we find the words of His mouth? In Psalm 19:7, David declares this, "Yahweh's law is perfect, restoring the soul. Yahweh's testimony is sure, making wise the simple."

Then, the apostle concludes his thought by the important phrase "redeeming the time." This term "redeem" in Greek refers to "paying a price, buying off, or making a ransom payment." In Galatians 3:13, Paul uses it to speak of Christ's redemption. He writes, "Christ redeemed us from the curse of the law, having become a curse for us. For it is written, "Cursed is everyone who hangs on a tree." Just as the Lord's death was the price paid to free us the judgment for our sin (the curse of the law), so we must also pay the price of time to live righteously. Before we received Christ, we lived in any fashion that we desired. Now is the moment to buy our time back and dedicate it to the Lord.

Then Paul adds this, "Because the days are evil." When it comes to our time, we cannot allow ourselves to act like those who do not believe in a living God. In Psalm 14:1, King David describes how an unwise person lives, "The fool has said in his heart, 'There is no God.' They are corrupt. They have done abominable deeds. There is no one who does good." Those who are unsaved live corruptly for themselves and do whatever they desire. Why? They do not believe in God. We are not to live like those who do not believe in God and live in any way that our heart would desire. We must live every moment in the light of God's presence. Why? The days are evil. We will be tempted to waste our "saved lives" on sinful activities or worthless deeds. These cannot bring any more than a temporary and unsatisfying solution to the difficult problems we must face. This is the world's way but not God's. We must redeem our time to find relief.

Evil is all around us and always tempting us to become distracted into what Solomon calls "striving after the wind." In Ecclesiastes 1:14, Solomon comments, "I have seen all the works that are done under the sun; and behold, all is vanity and a chasing after wind." The "works done under the sun" refers to all of the pursuit's humans engage in apart from God. These are all earthly endeavors. These are pursuits that cannot attain the things people want them to accomplish which is relief from their problems and the salvation of their eternal souls. It is as vain and useless a pursuit as trying to catch the wind. It cannot be obtained.

For us to simply add Jesus on a Sunday morning to these vain pursuits is even worse because we have the solutions inside us through His indwelling Spirit. We must change our pursuits to His. In 1 Corinthians 9:27, Paul calls the Christian life a race and emphatically declares, "Don't you know that those who run in a race all run, but one receives the prize? Run like that, that you may win." Like athletes running a long marathon race and facing many obstacles, we must run to win. We must run with the real intention, planning, and endurance it requires not only to finish the race but win it.

In verse 25-27, Paul describes how he was accomplishing this incredible feat, "Every man who strives in the games exercises self-control in all things. Now they do it to receive a corruptible crown, but we incorruptible. I therefore run like that, as not uncertainly [without aim]. I fight like that, as not beating the air, but I [Paul] beat my body and bring it into submission, lest by any means, after I have preached to others, I myself should be rejected." The word "strive" is a Greek word from which we derive the familiar English word "agonize." It denotes "strenuous effort to do something." The word translated "run" means "to exert one's full strength and commitment to perform something or perhaps overcome an obstacle." Paul was utilizing all his strength and resources in His "work" saving souls and building them up in the faith.

This required purpose, discipline, self-control, and the fight of his life. He pursued the Christian life intentionally with purpose rather than "uncertainty" or "without aim." He beat his body to bring his lusts, impulses, and desires into submission to his purpose. The word "beat" literally means to beat "black and blue." He boxed himself in order to stay on the path of right living. Why? He did not want to run unintentionally and box uselessly that in the end he had expended much effort without any spiritual gain. This kind of athlete will experience the calm, peace, joy, faith, comfort, hope, love, grace, courage, and trust we are searching for because he will sense that he is involved in something much bigger than himself - the race of the Christian life. When we walk unintentionally through life, we run aimlessly through a marathon and box only the air in the ring.

Imagine a long road throughout a town and countryside where there will be a marathon race. Before the race, many vendors from all over set up booths with each representing one of the delights or appetites of man whether wicked or just distracting. There are many foods and beer stands, sports activities, hobby shops, travel agents, prostitutes, and the list can go on and on. The runners become distracted and stop to enjoy the activities. In fact, some decide that they will spend their lives there and the time is foolishly wasted. Those who are managing the booths do not believe in the true God.

The Bible distinguishes between three kinds of activities on earth: righteous, wicked, and wasteful. When we became Christians, God forgave all our wicked deeds past, present, and future (Colossians 2:13-14). Christians have passed out of condemnation for these wicked deeds (Romans 8:1). Yet, Christians will have a judgment day where their other deeds will be judged. These deeds will involve the other two. In 2 Corinthians 5:10, Paul discusses these other rewards. He explains, "For we must all be revealed before the judgment seat of Christ; that each one may receive the things in the body, according to what he has done, whether good or bad." Here, Paul distinguishes between the only two types of our deeds that will be judged: good (righteous, holy actions) and bad (wasteful, useless actions). The Greek word translated "bad" is not the usual word used in the New Testament for evil, wickedness, or sin; rather, this word means "wasteful, worthless, and of no account." This would be in regard to the kingdom of God. It has no impact whatsoever.

We must keep this in mind as we redeem our time upon this earth. In James 4:14, he describes our lives as but a vapor that is here now and quickly gone. If we aren't careful, we will find ourselves at the end of our lives wondering why we did not do more for the Lord. Then we will discover that we were unwilling to walk intentionally. As a result, we became caught up in the useless activities of the world rather than the kingdom building activities of Christ. We will find that we pursued the pleasures and sins of the world.

In Colossians 4:5, Paul uses the same word to describe how we should interact with those outside the faith, "Walk in wisdom toward those who are outside, redeeming the time." Since the context is sharing the gospel, he is telling us to ransom the time with unbelievers by sharing and being an example of the gospel. We should not spend our time in the booths around the track but provide an alternative in Christ.

Living any way, we might desire will only leave us empty, fearful, tormented, in pain and anguish, desperate, regretful, guilty, aimless, anxious, and uncertain. Redeeming our time for Jesus produces a sense of calm, peace, joy, faith, comfort, hope, love, grace, courage, trust, and purpose.

To aid in this powerful endeavor of intentional living believers should recognize His presence daily. In order to redeem the time, Christians should acknowledge the Lord's presence as the manner of their lives. This means that they think, speak, and act as if Christ were viewing their every move, which He truly is. In Romans 12:1-2, the apostle Paul declares, "Therefore I urge you, brothers [all Christians], by the mercies of God, to present your bodies a living sacrifice, holy, acceptable to God, which is your spiritual service. Don't be conformed to this world, but be transformed by the renewing of your mind, so that you may prove what is the good, well-pleasing, and perfect will of God." Here, we are told to present our bodies, which are the part of us that does the speaking and acting, in spiritual service [worship word] to God. Paul contrasts the animal sacrifices that were given to the Lord in the Old Testament with the living sacrifice of ourselves in the New Testament.

This occurs by the renewing of our mind in the Word and prayer. When we read and study God's mind, heart, and commandments in the Bible and pray over its applications in our lives, this renews our minds and changes our thoughts to His mind and thoughts. This then prepares us to offer our words and actions to Him. Now, our time will matter. We will be cognizant of our thinking at any moment; therefore, we will speak and act like Christ and redeem the time.

In Proverbs 5:21, Solomon muses, "For the ways of man are before the eyes of Yahweh. He examines all his paths." First, the "He" could be the Lord examining a person's path. Or, second, the "he" could refer to the man realizing that the eyes of the Lord were watching him. So, he examines all his paths to make sure they were righteous before his God. If the first is true, then the second is certainly assumed. If the second is true, then the first is assumed. Either way, when a man's paths are examined, so is the time the man is spending on those paths. A man who is righteous would be involving himself primarily with righteous activities and not wasting his time in sinful or useless activities only.

How can we find the motivation to present our bodies, acknowledge His presence, and recognize His watchful eye? The simple answer is found in Psalm 63:8. Here, David cries out, "My soul clings to You; Your right hand upholds me." The king was running from his son who had taken over his kingdom. With his small band of loyal followers, he fled into the desert to hide and prepare a plan to retake his kingdom. The Hebrew word translated "cling" means to "cling, stick, stay close, cleave, keep close, stick to, stick with, follow closely, and join to." The word "upholds" refers to "grasping, holding, supporting, laying hold of, and holding fast to." During this difficult time, David was glued to the Lord and by faith claiming the Lord was holding him tight in His right hand. This represents the right hand of power (Matthew 26:64; Mark 14:62; Luke 22:69). The king was depending on God's power to support Him. Should we not do this very thing daily or must we wait for a difficult situation to come? Of course, the answer is obvious; it must be done daily.

Walking in His presence regularly can lessen or alleviate emptiness, fear, pain, guilt, regret, desperation, brokenness, aimlessness, uncertainty, or anxiety. They will fade away in the light of His presence. As we keep our eyes on Him, we can also redeem the time by dispensing of unnecessary time-consuming burdens. Now, this may be difficult to accept because we live in a pleasure-oriented society. This world of ours is filled with numerous possessions, pets, and activities for our joy and happiness. The bare necessities of living are overwhelming enough, let alone those burdens we add to our lives.

In Hebrews 12, after describing the many Old Testament examples of lives lived by faith, the author also uses the analogy of running a race. In verse 1, he says, "Therefore let us also, seeing we are surrounded by so great a cloud of witnesses [these lives lived by faith], lay aside every weight and the sin which so easily entangles us, and let us run with patience the race that is set before us."

For our discussion, we will focus on the phrase "lay aside every weight." The verb "lay aside" in the Greek speaks of "putting off, putting to the side, or putting away something." In Acts 7:58, Luke describes how the leaders, who were about to stone Stephen, had to take off their coats so they could be unencumbered in their efforts. In the same way, we should put off "every weight." This Greek word refers to "that which causes the arm to bend" meaning the carrying of a load. It is a general term used for something that will weigh us down. A runner strips himself of everything except what is necessary to win. This includes possessions, attitudes, and lifestyle that would encumber him from winning. He puts on the least amount of clothing and carries nothing in his hands. As for us, we must strip ourselves of any distractions and burdens that take our focus off Christ.

Remember what the apostle Paul says in 1 Corinthians 9 when our lives are compared to a race that we should desire to win. In verse 24, he writes this, "Don't you know that those who run in a race all run, but one receives the prize? Run like that, that you may win." We must have the goal of winning the race; that is, we want to become as close to the stature of Christ that we can. One of the sure ways that will slow us down (not running as far as we could) is by adding numerous unnecessary burdens to our life.

Practically, this means that we should take some serious time and make an assessment of our lives. Then, we should ask if we have made long term commitments that require far too much time to pay for, upkeep, utilize, or consider? Does it cause too much stress? Do we really need the pets, boats, vacation homes, hobbies, collections, sports, and clothes for ourselves, spouses, and children? These distract us from our real purpose on earth. They also add to our anxiety, stress, and frustration levels. These things require us to work longer hours and face long and difficult commutes. In John 15:19, Jesus declared this, "If you were of the world, the world would love its own; but because you are not of the world, but I chose you out of the world, because of this the world hates you." Notice just the first part. We have been chosen out of the world system by Jesus Christ.

In 1 John 2:15-16, the apostle John warns believers, "Don't love the world or the things that are in the world. If anyone loves the world, the Father's love isn't in him. For all that is in the world, the lust of the flesh, the lust of the eyes, and the pride of life, isn't the Father's, but is the worlds. The world is passing away with its lusts, but he who does God's will remains forever." The world offers us many pleasures which will satisfy our lusts and desires, but these will all pass away. It is only God's will (for us) that remains, and He has many important things for us to do for Him.

Another way to walk with spiritual intention is to allow others to help us. This might be a difficult one for many of us. Some do not like asking others for help or delegating responsibility to others to free up our time. We must either not take on the burdens in the first place or give some of the responsibility to others. In Acts 6:1-6, Luke mentions the apostles' struggle with tasks that they were not "called" to do. The historian describes the huge dilemma, "Now in those days, when the number of the disciples was multiplying, a complaint arose from the Hellenists against the Hebrews, because their widows were neglected in the daily service." Apparently, these Hellenists (Greek speaking Jews) thought that the Hebrews (Hebrew speaking Jews) were showing bias in the distribution of food to their needy causing a conflict.

As a result, the apostles realized that they couldn't spend their valuable time on tasks that they were not called to do and would have to find an appropriate solution. In verse 2-4, Luke continues, "The twelve summoned the multitude of the disciples and said, 'It is not appropriate for us to forsake the word of God and serve tables. Therefore, select from among you, brothers, seven men of good report, full of the Holy Spirit and of wisdom, [three qualifications] whom we may appoint over this business. But we will continue steadfastly in prayer and in the ministry of the word.'"

The leaders had to focus on the Word and prayer. So, they found capable people to whom they could delegate the other responsibilities. Afterward, they made sure that everyone involved was in agreement with their solution. In verses 5-6, it says, "Whose words pleased the whole multitude. They chose Stephen, a man filled with faith and of the Holy Spirit, [capable] Philip, Prochorus, Nicanor, Timon, Parmenas, and Nicolaus, a proselyte of Antioch; whom they set before the apostles. When they had prayed, they laid their hands on them" (DEJ). The problem was solved. They now had help.

Moses had to learn how to delegate also. In Exodus 18:13, Moses describes what happened, "On the next day, Moses sat to judge the people, and the people stood around Moses from the morning to the evening." Moses was there all day and every day resolving disputes among the people. In verse 14, his wife's father, Jethro, stepped in to give some advice, "When Moses' father-in-law saw all that he did to the people, he said, 'What is this thing that you do for the [God's] people? Why do you sit alone, and all the people stand around you from morning to evening?'" He couldn't understand why Moses was doing everything by himself. He needed to concentrate in ruling Israel does not deal with every dispute.

In verses 15-16, Moses attempted an explanation, "Moses said to his father-in-law, 'Because the people come to me to inquire of God. When they have a matter, they come to me, and I judge between a man and his neighbor, and I make them know the statutes of God, and his laws.'" He believed that he was the only one who could do the job. In verses 17-18, Jethro responds with his own view, "Moses' father-in-law said to him, 'The thing that you do is not good. You will surely wear away, both you, and this people that is with you; for the thing is too heavy for you. You are not able to perform it yourself alone.'" He urged Moses to consider the fact that he would eventually wear himself out. The people would eventually grow weary also. The task was too heavy for one man to bear. It was not good.

In verses 19-20, Jethro made a suggestion, "Listen now to my voice. I will give you counsel, and God be with you. You [Moses] represent the people [Israel] before God and bring the causes to God. You shall teach them the statutes and the laws and shall show them the way in which they must walk, and the work that they must do." First, he had to teach God's laws to those who would take on the responsibility.

Second, Moses had to select spiritually mature, capable and respected people and let them do the bulk of the work. In verses 21-22, Jethro asserts, "Moreover you shall provide out of all the people able men which fear God: men of truth, hating unjust gain; and place such over them, to be rulers of thousands, rulers of hundreds, rulers of fifties, and rulers of tens. Let them judge the people at all times. It shall be that every great matter they shall bring to you, but every small matter they shall judge themselves. So shall it be easier for you, and they shall share the load with you." Here, he tells Moses to only take on the most serious matters and leave everything else up to the delegated leaders to decide. He did not need to know all the details of every single case. He had bigger matters to look after.

He indicates that Moses should inquire of the Lord and describes the results. In verse 23, it says, "If you will do this thing, and God commands you so, then you will be able to endure, and all these people also will go to their place in peace." This delegation of responsibility and better use of his time will make it easier for him to be a leader. This will also bring peace to his people because their issues will be taken care of in a timely manner. Through these examples, we see that we concentrate on growing and get help for the rest.

In our old lives, our time was our own and now it is His. To dedicate our time to Him, it is necessary to change from unintentional living to an intentional one. This encourages growth that can lead to overcoming the emptiness, torment, pain, desperation, brokenness, despair, anxiety, aimlessness, regret, guilt, or uncertainty we are feeling. Let us get on with the business of building the kingdom of God and find relief.

Chapter 3

Study Scripture Consistently

In this chapter, we will consider the life-sustaining critical importance of God's Word, the Scriptures. Once saved, some problems may fade in the light of this new relationship with the Lord. Others may persist and must be dealt with through the consistent living of the Christian life. As old challenges linger or new ones arise, our emptiness, desperation, fear, pain, regret, guilt, despair, anxiety, lack of purpose, concern over finances, or sense of doom might rear their ugly heads again. Then, the consistent living of the Christian life will help to release our captive hearts and bring them calm, peace, joy, faith, comfort, hope, love, grace, courage, purpose, and trust flooding into them.

One of the elements our Christian walk is the reading, studying, and applying of the principles found in the Bible. As we grow in our knowledge of God and live according to His blueprint in His Word, we will become more successful in handling the issues that come our way. Jesus was able to deal with the many difficulties He faced and the more we become like Him, the more we will do the same. The major method used by God for transforming us into His image is through the Scriptures. The Word is life-transcending, life-giving, and life-changing. This should compel us to become absorbed in it. To understand how paramount God's Word is, we should understand that God is not like us. He is far beyond us.

In Isaiah 55, God speaks directly to the people of Israel through Isaiah, the prophet. In Isaiah 55:8-9, he writes, "'For my thoughts are not your thoughts, and your ways are not my ways,' says Yahweh. 'For as the heavens are higher than the earth, so are my ways higher than your ways, and my thoughts than your thoughts.'" This passage indicates that our natural ways of seeing life are not always correct. They are not always in line with God's ways because His ways are higher.

In fact, our "ways", often gets us into trouble. Solomon writes in Proverbs 16:25 "There is a way which seems right to a man, but in the end, it leads to death." Jeremiah utters in Jeremiah 17:9 "The heart is deceitful above all things, and it is exceedingly corrupt: who can know it?" Rather than lead us away from our emptiness, desperation, fear, pain, regret, guilt, despair, anxiety, purposelessness, financial worry, or doom and gloom, it can add to it. We can't always trust our hearts or our intuition or what makes sense or seems right to us to determine the best way of solving problems; instead, we must know God's thoughts and ways, which are higher, because he is the author of all life and ought to know how we should live.

And where do we find these ways? In Hebrews 1: 1-2, the inspired author asserts, "God, having in the past spoken to the fathers [of the Jewish nation] through the prophets at many times and in various ways, has at the end of these days spoken to us by his Son, whom he appointed heir of all things, through whom also he made the world." In the Holy Bible, the Old Testament is God speaking His thoughts and ways to the fathers in the prophets. The New Testament is the same God speaking His thoughts and ways in His Son (delivered through His apostles and prophets}. So, the Lord God's thoughts and ways are in the Scriptures.

In 2 Peter 1:20-21, Peter declared, "Knowing this first, that no prophecy of Scripture is of private interpretation. For no prophecy ever came by the will of man: but holy men of God spoke, being moved by the Holy Spirit." When the apostle speaks of this "prophecy of Scripture" here, he is speaking of the entire Scriptures, not just the part written by prophets. All the writers of the Old and New Testaments of the Bible were "moved" by the Spirit to speak.

The Greek word translated "moved" means "to bring, or to be carried along." A good illustration of this word's use is found in Acts 27:15. In this passage, when Luke described the apostle Paul's voyage to Rome, he said that the ship Paul was on encountered a violent wind. Instead of sailing against it, "we gave way to it, and were driven along." The word translated by two words in the English "driven along" is the exact same word, but it is used in a physical way. Inspiration involved "being driven along" in their writing by the Spirit.

The holy writers of Scripture allowed themselves in some supernatural way to be driven along by the Holy Spirit, so the end result was their words but also the very words of God. The Bible contains God's thoughts and ways, not our human wisdom written by men who were pretending to be from God. It is God's wisdom written by men speaking from God. Not one word originates from man's own human will and own human thoughts alone. That is Peter's point.

The apostle Paul reiterates this in 2 Timothy 3:16 when he says, "All scripture is inspired by God." This Greek term translated "inspired" comes from two Greek words: one meaning "God" and the other "to breathe." Therefore, the term is "God-breathed." The Spirit of God "breathed" into their minds producing His very thoughts and words as they wrote the Scriptures.

It is interesting that the latter Greek word can also mean "to blow" like the "blowing of the wind." When John relates the story of the Lord Jesus walking on the water in John 6:18, he describes the scene in these words, "The Sea was tossed by a great wind blowing." John, the apostle, uses the same word. In a sense, the Lord God "blows men along like the wind." This fits perfectly with the description of Peter. Once again, the writers of the Scriptures allowed themselves in some supernatural way to be driven along by the "wind" of the Holy Spirit, so the end result was more than just their words; instead, they were the very words of God.

These are beautiful descriptions of how God, in a life-transcending way, brings His thoughts and ways to us in the sacred writings. So, from Genesis to Revelation, the Almighty is speaking His thoughts and ways. Scripture transcends this earthly life. It is supernatural in every way. And this God-breathed book contains what we need to know spiritually to live the way God desires and be transformed into Christ's image resulting in hearts filled with calm, peace, joy, faith, comfort, hope, love, grace, courage, purpose, and trust.

In 2 Peter 1:2-3, Peter describes this in these words, "Grace to you and peace be multiplied in the knowledge of God and of Jesus our Lord, seeing that his divine power has granted to us all things that pertain to life and godliness, through the knowledge of him [God] who called us by his own glory and virtue." Every single thing we will need that pertains to life and godliness (this life and holy living the way God desires) will come through the knowledge of Him (His thoughts and ways). And where do we find that knowledge of Him? Once again, it is in the Bible.

But notice, it comes with or is granted to us by "divine power." With that knowledge comes the power to act on it. The Greek word translated "power" is the root of our English word "dynamite." It speaks of extreme, explosive, mighty power. This power is divine, supernatural power. It is the power of deity energizing us to change.

Paul speaks of this power in his letter to Thessalonica. He had only been in the city for a very short time, but the gospel (God's Word) had had an explosively powerful effect on the people there. In 1 Thessalonians 1:5, he declares this, "And that our Good News came to you not in word only, but also in power, and in the Holy Spirit, and with much assurance. You know what kind of men we showed ourselves to be among you for your sake." The gospel came in word (in this case, His thoughts and ways on how to become a Christian), power, and the Holy Spirit. The Word of God transforms lives because it contains divine words with divine power.

Not only is it powerful but it is our spiritual nourishment for our growth in Him. After we come to Christ, we need to nourish ourselves in the Word. We have to be fed spiritually through God's Word throughout the rest of our lives. In 1 Peter 2:1-2, the apostle proclaimed, "Putting away therefore all wickedness, all deceit, hypocrisies, envies, and all evil speaking, as newborn babies, long for the pure milk of the Word, that with it you may grow." He says we should put away our sinful ways and start longing for the Word so we can grow in Christ.

Have you ever been in the presence of a newborn baby who is hungry and wants his or her milk? There is nothing like the blood-curdling scream of a desperate newborn. The baby's desire must be satisfied as soon as possible or there will be no peace. Interesting enough, Peter used this analogy for our longing for the nourishment of the Word.

In 1 Timothy 4:6, Paul emphasizes this very same concept when he writes to young Pastor Timothy, "If you instruct the brothers of these things, you will be a good servant of Christ Jesus, nourished in the words of the faith, and of the good doctrine which you have followed." The words of faith and sound doctrine are the truths of the scriptures.

33

This Bible is our nourishment, and we are to constantly be reading, studying, and applying it to grow. And while we are nourishing ourselves on God's Word, it is doing its work in us. It is changing us. It will clear our hearts of the fear, pain, emptiness, desperation, regret, guilt, despair, anxiety, lack of purpose, or concern over finances and fill them with calm, peace, joy, faith, comfort, hope, courage, love, grace, purpose, and trust.

The Word is life changing. In Isaiah 55:10-11, the prophet declares, "For as the rain comes down and the snow from the sky, and doesn't return there, but waters the earth, and makes it grow and bud, and gives seed to the sower and bread to the eater; so is my word that goes out of my mouth: it will not return to me void, but it will accomplish that which I [God] please, and it will prosper in the thing I sent it to do."

God sends forth his Word into our lives to accomplish His purpose, it will not return empty. In 1 Thessalonians 2:13, Paul discusses the same concept when he says, "For this because we also thank God without ceasing, that, when you received from us the word of the message of God, you accepted it not as the word of men, but, as it is in truth, the word of God, which also works in you who believe." The "accomplishment of God's purpose" or "the work" the Word performs in our lives is the changing of our old unrighteous thoughts and ways to God's righteous thoughts and ways.

Due to our flesh, this is not easy for us. God requires us, as Christians, to live supernaturally upon this natural earth. He sometimes asks us to think and behave in ways that seem contrary to everything we hold true. These are thoughts and ways higher than us like "love your enemies" (Matthew 5:44) or "forgive someone seventy times seven" (Matthew 18:22). Who can do that? Of course, it is impossible without God's divine power unleashed through his Word in His Holy Spirit

34

which "does its work in us." Then, we are changed into the likeness of Christ because our Savior and Lord loves His enemies and forgives us seventy times seven. These are just two examples of the many ways in which we should become like Jesus Christ. This cannot be accomplished unless we are consistently in the Word of God.

This is the reason the Scriptures speak to so many areas of life because so many areas have to change to become like our Lord Jesus. And the Word provides everything we need for life and godliness including the solutions to our problems. It does this by providing God's thoughts and ways concerning the knowledge of Him, His Son, and Spirit. It provides God's blueprints or principles for Christian living showing us how to relate to each other (1 John 4:7-12), the world (James 4:4), our spouses (Colossians 3:18-21), children (Ephesians 6:1-4), the government (Romans 13:1-8), and the church (1 Timothy 3:15). These are just a few of them.

The Scriptures convicts of sin when we are not following His ways. Hebrews 4:12 says, "For the word of God is living and active, and sharper than any two-edged sword, piercing even to the dividing of soul and spirit, of both joints and marrow, and is able to discern the thoughts and intentions of the heart." Have you ever felt the Word speaking to you so directly that it feels as if it is reaching deeply into your soul and convicting you of a specific sin only you and God know about? I have numerous times. That's why it's a "living and active" Word. It is always relevant and active. We don't have to make it relevant and active. It already speaks to every generation and is activated when it is read.

The Bible provides the power to overcome that sin. Psalm 119:11 declares, "I have hidden your word in my heart, that I might not sin against you." Also, it can provide comfort in time of trouble. In Psalm 119:28, the inspired writer states,

"My soul is weary with sorrow: strengthen me according to your word." Then in verse 50, he writes, "This is my comfort in my affliction, for your word has revived me." The Word of God has power to turn the sorrows, troubles, and difficulties we face into triumphs of great hope, joy, calm, peace, faith, comfort, love, grace, courage, purpose, and trust. How? His word must permeate our thoughts, words, and actions.

So, one way to grow in our Christian lives is to study the Scriptures consistently. We need to read the Bible itself. It is important to read books, listen to sermons, and even sing about the Word, but this cannot replace the reading of it for us. The power is in the Word itself as the Holy Spirit works through it. In Colossians 3:16, Paul encourages the church to make the Word a key part of their lives. He writes, "Let the word of Christ dwell in you richly; in all wisdom teaching and admonishing one another with psalms, hymns, and spiritual songs, singing with grace in your heart to the Lord." The Greek word translated "dwell" comes from the root word meaning "house." It carries the idea of taking up residence within someone. The Word of God must take up residence within us. It must become a critical part of our lives.

Some people think the Bible is too hard to understand, so they don't read it. There certainly are some parts that are hard to understand, even Peter acknowledged this (2 Peter 3:16). But remember, the Bible was written to the common man, not to pastors (except the letters to Timothy and Titus). Here's the key: the more we read it, the easier it becomes to understand. Did we not have to read textbook chapters more than once in school to really understand them? How much more chapters of the Bible written by God? Dabbling in the Word will not produce the life-changing power I'm talking about. We have to go deep into God's Word. How do we do this? We must develop a routine. Life will constantly crowd out commitment to the Word, unless we create a time and place to read it. We are creatures of habit, and we must create a specific routine for reading the Word of God, which is a practice we cannot live without.

Next, we must find a reliable translation. We have to do some research to determine the most competent translation to use. The most popular are not always the best. We will want one that translates the original languages faithfully to our language. A translation that is a little stiffer in its literal meaning is better than one that is looser. This way we know exactly what the Bible says, not what someone thinks it says.

We should begin with one of the gospels and imagine that we are walking along the road in the first century with Jesus. We should listen to what He says and watch what He does by examining what the writers said about who He was and why He came. This is the person we have put our faith in for salvation, and we must get to know Him.

Once we have done this, we must find a pastor-teachers to instruct us in the deeper truths of the Scriptures. You see, God has placed within the church evangelists and pastor-teachers. The responsibility of the evangelist is to equip the saints to share the gospel. This will build the body up numerically. The responsibility of the pastor-teacher is to instruct the saints in sound doctrine. This will build the church up spiritually. In Ephesians 4:11-12, the apostle Paul describes this principle, "He gave some to be apostles; and some, prophets; [these saints laid the foundation and have now passed away] and some, evangelists; and some, shepherds and teachers [these saints remain today]." The term "shepherds and teachers" refers to only one person. These shepherd-teachers shepherd the flock by teaching them. Paul continues to explain their purpose by saying, "For the perfecting of the saints, to the work of serving, to the building up of the body of Christ." This perfecting and building are toward spiritual maturity.

In Ephesians 4:13, Paul explains that their goal is for the saints to become fully mature to the point that they measure up to Christ's stature. In verse 14, he contrasts this maturity to immaturity or childlike behavior. He describes spiritual children (those who are not shepherd-taught) as ones who are "tossed back and forth and carried about with every wind of doctrine, by the trickery of men, in craftiness, after the wiles of error." Children go from spiritual fad to spiritual fad. They cannot land on any one truth because they do not know the truth well enough. The pastor-teacher's duty is to diligently study the Word of God and teach it to the flock of God by presenting it to them clearly and completely.

Paul taught Timothy this important responsibility in his letters to this pastor and son in the faith. In 1 Timothy 4:11, Paul gives Timothy a series of injunctions and then writes, "Command and teach these things." Then, in verse 13, Paul adds, "Until I come, pay attention to reading, to exhortation, and to teaching." In verse 15, he continues, "Be diligent in these things." In 1 Timothy 6:2, again he encourages, "Teach and exhort these things." In 2 Timothy 1:13-14, the apostle Paul encourages Timothy, "Hold the pattern of sound words which you have heard from me, in faith and love which is in Christ Jesus. That good thing, which was committed to you, guard through the...Spirit who dwells in us." Pastors should be teaching sound doctrine from their church pulpits so the saints can grow in deeper ways. This kind of instruction will require much more time on their parts.

So, as we begin the journey of finding a true church to be a part of, we need someone in the pulpit who can preach the deeper truths of God's Word soundly and correctly. If we can't find this kind of preacher, then we will have to listen to one on the radio or social media. It is the deeper truths that can speak directly to the issues we face not simply the basic truths of God's love and mercy. God is so much more than just a God of love and mercy. There is much more he desires from us than to just "trust Him" and endure all the challenges we are facing.

Once we develop some real consistency in the Word, we should live it constantly. In James 1:22-24, the brother of Jesus put it this way, "But be doers of the word, and not only hearers, deluding your own selves. For if anyone is a hearer of the word and not a doer, he is like a man looking at his natural face in a mirror; for he sees himself, and goes away, and immediately forgets what kind of man he was." He says the Word is like a mirror in which we see our true selves sometimes good, sometimes not so good. Nevertheless, it is our true selves.

When the Word shows us areas where we have reached Christlikeness, we can praise God. When the Word convicts us of sin or demonstrates how we need to behave in a certain area of life, we need to act on it, not forget about it and go on with our lives. We need to read it and heed it. How do we do this? We should read the Scriptures in order to grow in our knowledge of Jesus and to understand the principles that the Lord God desires us to follow.

This will be found primarily in the various letters of the New Testament. The Lord's apostles had the responsibility to deliver the revealed truth of God from Christ through their teaching and eventually their writing. This includes Paul who was an apostle of a different kind. The gospels are biographies of Jesus, the book of Acts is an historical account, and the last book of the Bible (Revelation) is the prophecies of future events. These inspired writings contain many principles of living, but it is in the letters that we will find the most. This is important to know because some feel that the words of Jesus are the only ones to heed. This could not be further from the truth.

39

The apostles taught their doctrine systematically and their letters were responses to the people's misunderstandings, misbehavior, and errors that had crept into the church. The letters were written to correct them. Usually, they are taught in sections or passages devoted to a topic addressing one of these issues. As a result, it would be best to read Romans to Jude five times. While reading these letters, highlight verses that provide principles for living. This is especially critical in the areas in which you might be struggling.

At first, as a new believer in Christ, you do not have to be concerned with any sections that are hard to understand. Once this is done, we should practice applying the many commands, especially in current relationships. For example, we might come across a passage such as Romans 13:1. The author writes, "Let every soul be in subjection to the higher authorities [police, etc.], for there is no authority except from God, and those who exist are ordained by God." Perhaps, we drive too fast. We might begin to slow down and follow the law. This honors the Lord. We cannot follow every principle every moment but should take one at a time and work on it. Above all else, we should allow ourselves to make mistakes and plenty of time to grow.

Once the Scriptures are being studied consistently and lived constantly, believers should begin sharing it persistently. Since we have been highlighting verses with principles of living, we should be ready to use them in our lives. First, we could begin sharing the Scriptures with our family. In Deuteronomy 6:7, concerning the commandments of the Lord God, Moses told the Almighty's people, "And you shall teach them diligently to your children, and shall talk of them when you sit in your house, and when you walk by the way...when you lie down, and when you rise up." Though speaking about a father to his children, the general principle is clear. The Bible's truths are to be shared with everyone in our families.

We should be using the Scriptures daily with our spouses and other family members as we live our lives with them. In Joshua 1:8-9, when Joshua stood before the Lord God as he was about to enter Canaan, the Almighty gave him this command, "This book of the law shall not depart from your mouth, but you shall meditate on it day and night, that you may observe to do according to all that is written in it; for then you shall make your way prosperous, and...you shall have good success. Haven't I commanded you? Be strong and courageous. Don't be afraid. Don't be dismayed, for Yahweh your God is with you wherever you go." When we follow this command, we need to bring the ones closest to us down the same path.

Second, insert these verses into casual conversation. One of the great testimonies we can have been found in our constant and continual joy amid a many of life's difficult challenges. That joy can come from God's Word and shared with others in casual interaction. In Psalm 19:8, the psalmist writes this, "Yahweh's precepts are right, rejoicing the heart. Yahweh's commandment is pure, enlightening the eyes." The author of Psalm 119:111 cries out, "I have taken your testimonies as a heritage forever, for they are the joy of my heart." So, we can spread that joy by spreading His Word everywhere we go.

Third, we should always share the Word in any ministry or service we might become involved in. The apostles spoke of their ministry in service in Acts 6:4, when they said, "But we will continue steadfastly in prayer and in the ministry of the word." The ministry of the apostles was to evangelize the world and minister to the saints, and they used two tools; they were prayer and the Word of God. These are sufficient, and we have the same mandate.

Many had come into the Corinthian church relying on their own skills in persuasion to move the people away from the truth and into error. In 1 Corinthians 2:4-5, Paul contrasts this with how he ministered, "My speech and my preaching were not in persuasive words of human wisdom, but in demonstration of the [Holy] Spirit and of power, that your faith wouldn't stand in the wisdom of men, but in the power of God." The apostle relied on God's Word, which comes with great power, not on human wisdom and persuasion. We must do the same in our speaking and service.

The Word of God is the blueprint by which we live. It is the map for a believer's actions in God's grace for spiritual growth. It took God thousands of years to produce it and required the involvement of many prophets, apostles, and even the Son of God Himself. We must read it, live it, and share it. It is a key solution to the difficulties and challenges we face. As we learn, apply, and share more about God, the Father, the Son, and the Spirit and how to live according to His principles, we should experience more and more calm, peace, joy, faith, comfort, hope, love, grace, courage, trust, and purpose.

Chapter 4

Persist in Watchful Prayer

Though much of the issues we now face can be settled at our salvation, we still have a long life upon the earth which possesses many more obstacles. These challenges can still cause emptiness, fearfulness, pain, regret, guilt, desperation, despair, aimlessness, anxiety, or uncertainty to return. One of the ways in which we can find freedom in the midst of these difficult moments is to develop a consistent prayer life. This can release our captive hearts from this slavery and fill our hearts with peace, calm, joy, faith, comfort, hope, love, grace, courage, purpose, and trust.

How does this happen? As we read the Word of God, He literally speaks to us. As we pray, we speak to Him. Prayer is the most intimate kind of communion with God. Prayer and the Word is the process of communication between God and man. In 1 John 5:14, the apostle John describes prayer as boldly speaking "before" Him. The Greek word connotes a face-to-face interaction with God that we have as believers. Therefore, prayer is coming to the throne of our God and standing face to face before the Father.

We can utilize this time simply to talk things over with our God. We can talk about feelings, struggles, or whatever else we desire. In Psalm 5:2, the psalmist prays, "Listen to the voice of my cry, my King and my God; for to you do I pray." Later, in Psalm 34:15, the psalmist says, "Yahweh's eyes are toward the righteous. His ears listen to their cry." We speak and He listens. We share our inner most feelings and He hears us. Of course, these inevitably become petitions for us or others. He wants His people to bring everything they need before Him.

This is exactly what our God desires. In Psalm 62:8, David describes it this way, "Trust in him at all times, you people. Pour out your heart before him. God is a refuge for us." He is ready for us to bring anything we are facing to His throne (Psalm 5:2; 6:9; 17:1; 39:12; 54:2).

As problems and negative feelings flare up in our lives, we must depend upon Him for help, guidance, and release in prayer. In 1 Peter 5:6-7, Peter explains this truth, "Humble yourselves therefore under the mighty hand of God, that he may exalt you in due time; casting all your worries on him, because he cares for you." Notice, the last phrase, "he cares for you" is literally "it matters." Not only does God love us but our cares and concerns matter to Him. These are never ignored but are heard and answered by Him.

Answers may come in a variety of forms. First, we will see answers exactly as we prayed for them. In Acts 12, Peter was imprisoned, the saints were praying for him, and God freed Him. In verse 5, Luke wrote, "Peter therefore was kept in the prison, but constant prayer was made by the assembly to God for him." The word "constant" is better translated "fervently or intensely." Every minute Peter sat chained in that prison was met with a minute of intense crying out to the Lord God for his deliverance. And then, the answer came. Suddenly, an angel appeared in Peter's cell and the chains that held him fell to the ground without awakening the guards. Peter walked past the four of them and out of the prison. The large iron-gate, which led into the city, opened on its own accord, and Peter was free.

Peter went immediately to notify these saints. In verses 12-16, Luke recorded what happened next, "Thinking about that, he came to the house of Mary, the mother of John who was called Mark, where many were gathered together, and they were praying. When Peter knocked at the door of the gate, a maid named Rhoda came to answer [the door]. When she recognized Peter's voice, she didn't open the gate for joy, but ran in, and reported that Peter was standing in front of the gate. They said to her, 'You are crazy!' But she insisted that it was so. They said, 'It is his angel.' But Peter continued knocking. When they had opened, they saw him and were amazed." God can and will answer our prayers.

Second, we may see answers that are different, but all will be for our good or the good of others. In Romans 8:28, Paul asserts, "We know that all things work together for good for those who love God, to those who are called according to his purpose." This includes answers to our prayers. The Lord was in the Garden of Gethsemane. In Matthew 28:39, in His humanity, Jesus asks the Father to allow Him to forego the cross. The apostle writes, "He went forward a little, fell on his face, and prayed, saying, 'My Father, if it is possible, let this cup pass away from me; nevertheless, not what I desire, but what you desire.'" He knew God's will was to save the world, so for the good of others, the Father could not answer His prayers in the exact way He desired. Plus, great glory was awaiting Him afterward.

Third, some answers may not bring the full deliverance from physical problems or difficult circumstances, but God will provide the comfort, peace, and patience we will need to endure it. In 2 Corinthians 12, Paul explained that he had received some powerful revelations. Since the Lord was concerned that he would become prideful, he sent a thorn in the flesh, which was a messenger of Satan. God allowed the Devil to strike Him (most likely with a physical malady) to keep Him humble. He prayed three times, but the Lord God refused to remove the problem. So, Paul learned the power of God's grace to endure. In verse 9, Paul describes the Lord God's answer, "He has said to me, 'My grace is sufficient for you, for my power is made perfect in weakness.' Most gladly therefore I [Paul] will rather glory in my weaknesses, that the power of Christ may rest on me.'" Paul accepted God's grace as an answer and found relief. We must do the same.

Fourth, we can be sure that all answers will be for the purpose of glorifying God's Son and advancing the kingdom either numerically or spiritually. The Philippians had prayed for Paul since the church was established. When Paul was arrested and sent to Rome, they were fearful and worried. They could not understand why the Lord God allowed him to be imprisoned in the first place and then to go on trial before the emperor. This often happens to us. We cannot understand what God is doing when he does not deliver us or a loved one from a physical malady or difficult situation. One reason is this: God wants the gospel shared to someone who may not have access to the salvation message.

In Philippians 1, Paul encourages them by explaining the "good" that was coming from it. In verse 12-15, Paul states, "Now I want you to know, brothers and sisters, that what has happened to me has actually served to [pioneer] advance the gospel. As a result, it has become clear throughout the whole palace guard and to everyone else that I am in chains for Christ. And because of my chains, most of the brothers and sisters have become confident in the Lord and dare all the more to proclaim the gospel without fear. It is true that some preach Christ out of envy and rivalry, but others out of goodwill." The gospel was being shared by him to Caesar's household (servants, perhaps family members), the guards he was chained to, and eventually even the emperor himself. Also, the Lord had awakened a sleeping church to become bold again to advance the kingdom.

The word translated "advance" in the English meant to make a pioneer advance where the gospel had not been. It was utilized by the Roman military to describe the soldiers who would cut away trees, plants, and shrubs to build a road for the army to advance in wartime. Since Paul's imprisonment, the gospel was making a pioneer advance into the capital city. The Lord God did not answer their prayers for Paul's deliverance because he was to make a pioneer advance of the gospel. This perspective brought him peace.

Fifth, all answers will bring peace from God as we accept whatever He does according to His will. In Philippians 4:6-7, Paul writes this powerful statement, "In nothing be anxious, but in everything, by prayer and petition with thanksgiving, let your requests be made known to God. And the peace of God, which surpasses all understanding, will guard your hearts and your thoughts in Christ Jesus." Whatever issues we face, struggles we have, hurdles we must overcome, we should bring them to God in prayer. Then we should thank Him for the privilege of coming before the throne and the answer He will provide. This brings peace. As we saw in 1 Peter 5, we can rest in His care. Yet, we must remember, He does all things according to His will. Paul writes these words in his letter to Ephesus, "In whom also we were assigned an inheritance, having been foreordained according to the purpose of him who does all things after the counsel of his will" (Ephesians 1:11).

Sixth, God will not give us what we desire if it is sinful or from sinful motives. Among the readers of the letter James wrote, there were members of the church who were fighting among themselves over the satisfaction of their own lusts. In James 4:1-3, the half-brother of Jesus admonishes the saints, "Where do wars and fightings among you come from? Don't they come from your pleasures that war in your members? You lust, and don't have. You murder and covet, and can't obtain. You fight and make war [with one another]. You don't have, because you don't ask [pray]. You ask and don't receive, because you ask with wrong motives, so that you may spend it for your pleasures." As we can see, the Lord will not answer these kinds of prayers.

Praying is a critical part of the Christian life, and we need to pray consistently. Prayer must become an intricate part of our lives. In Colossians 4:2, Paul said, "Continue steadfastly in prayer, watching therein with thanksgiving." In 2 Timothy 1:3, Paul describes his prayers for Timothy as "unceasing." In 1 Thessalonians 3:10, he described his intercession for them, "Night and day praying exceedingly that we may see your face, and may perfect that which is lacking in your faith?" Finally, 1 Thessalonians 5:17, Paul commands, "Pray without ceasing." The point isn't that we have to pray every minute of every day; but instead, prayer has to be an important part of our lives. Here are several steps Christians might take that will definitely help them develop powerful prayer lives.

It is important that we as Christians develop the habit of praying. Our prayer must become a pattern or practice in a Christian's life. Of course, it will happen naturally when we encounter crises, but it should become a regular part of our lives. This is done by developing the habit of praying. The Lord Jesus had a practice or specific pattern of prayer. In Matthew 14:23, the apostle describes what happened after the feeding of the five thousand, "After he had sent the multitudes away, he went up into the mountain by himself to pray. When evening had come, he was there alone."

In Mark 1:35, Mark records, "Early in the morning, while it was still dark, he rose up and went out, and departed into a deserted place, and prayed there." In Luke 5:16, the historian asserts, "But he withdrew himself into the desert, and prayed." In these passages, it becomes obvious that the Lord went to a quiet place to pray alone for a period of time usually before or after the events of the day. This was His consistent habit or practice throughout His ministry.

How can we do this? Notice, that Jesus took the initiative and sent the people around Him away. He did not just allow things to happen but made sure He had the time to devote to prayer. We must do the same. This does not have to be done in a quiet room. We could adapt it to our own personalities, schedules, and even interests. Some take long walks and pray. Others speak to the Lord while driving to work. Still others enjoy their communication with the Lord in bed. We have the freedom to choose the times and places we pray. The main issue is for Christians to be praying regularly.

One way in which we can organize our prayer time is by structuring it around biblical themes. Believers could move from one theme to another or subject to subject in our prayers. These prayers usually encompass the topics of confession, praise and thanksgiving, personal petitions and intercession, then watching and waiting. Another idea would be to record the prayer requests for ourselves in a book or journal. Then, we could write down the numerous answers that God may give, and this could become a part of our time in praise and thanksgiving.

First, we should spend time in the confession of our sins. This is a time to purify our hearts before God. In 1 John 1:9, the apostle declares, "If we confess our sins, he is faithful and righteous to forgive us the sins, and to cleanse us from all unrighteousness." This is not the once for all forgiveness for our sins we receive at salvation but the confession of sins that restores our relationship with God.

In the book of Psalms, David provides a simple pattern. In Psalm 139:23-24, David asks the Lord to search him and reveal his sins, "Search me, God, and know my heart. Try me, and know my thoughts. See if there is any wicked way in me, and lead me in the everlasting way." In Psalm 26:2, David cries, "Examine me, Yahweh, and prove me. Try my heart and my mind." Though the Lord regularly convicts us of sin, we should ask the Lord to examine us and convict us of any sins that have gone unrecognized.

In Psalm 51:1-4, David provides a simple dialogue we can have with God. After the grievous sin of adultery, he pleads with the Lord, "Have mercy on me, God, according to your loving kindness. According to the multitude of your tender mercies, blot out my transgressions. Wash me thoroughly from my iniquity. Cleanse me from my sin. For I know my transgressions. My sin is constantly before me. Against you, and you only, have I sinned, and done that which is evil in your sight; that you may be proved right when you speak, and justified when you judge."

Second, we can praise God for who He is and thank Him for what He has done. In Psalm 7:17, the psalmist writes, "I will give thanks to Yahweh according to his righteousness, and will sing praise to the name of Yahweh Most High." In Psalm 30:12, the writer adds, "To the end that my heart may sing praise to you, and not be silent. Yahweh my God, I will give thanks to you forever!" In Psalm 100:4, the composer shouts, "Enter into his gates with thanksgiving, into his courts with praise. Give thanks to him, and bless his name."
So, both praise and thanksgiving are appropriate in prayer.

Praise usually centers on His "Name." This refers to all that He is, which includes His attributes. We might praise Him for His love, grace, mercy, power, justice and others that we see described in the Scriptures or in our lives as He works. Our thanksgiving expresses our gratitude for His blessings. In Psalm 26:7, the psalmist declares, "That I may make the voice of thanksgiving to be heard, and tell of all your wondrous deeds." In Psalm 33:2, the inspired writer pens, "Give thanks to Yahweh with the lyre. Sing praises to him with the harp of ten strings."

Third, we can come before God to ask Him for help on behalf of ourselves and others. Both are in the songbook and prayers of Israel. First, we see personal petitions. In Psalm 22:11, it says, "Don't be far from me, for trouble is near. For there is no one to help." Then in verse 19, he writes, "But don't be far off, Yahweh. You are my help: hurry to help me.' In Psalm 40:13, the psalmist composes these words, "Be pleased, Yahweh, to deliver me. Hurry to help me, Yahweh."

Also, we have intercessory prayers for others written in the psalms. In Psalm 6:4, it says, "Return, Yahweh. Deliver my soul, and save me for your loving kindness' sake." Then in Psalm 7:1, the author entreats, "Yahweh, my God, I take refuge in you. Save me from all those who pursue me, and deliver me." These are simple pleas, and we can make them as detailed and elaborate as we desire.

Finally, there is watching and waiting. This means that we pray and watch for God's answer. It may take some time and so we should be patient. In Psalm 5:3, David explains this watching in prayer, "Yahweh, in the morning you shall hear my voice. In the morning I will lay my requests before you, and will watch expectantly." In Psalm 59:9, it states, "Oh, my Strength, I watch for you, for God is my high tower." Then we should wait and continue to pray. In Psalm 25:5, the writer says, "Guide me in your truth, and teach me, for you are the God of my salvation, I wait for you all day long."

In Psalm 27:14, the psalmist pens, "Wait for Yahweh. Be strong...let your heart take courage. Yes, wait for Yahweh." Psalm 130:5 says, "I wait for Yahweh. My soul waits. I hope in his word." To pray, I simply begin with, "Father, I am so sorry for..." and "Father, I praise you for..." This is an easy structure to help us get started in building a prayer life. I have used this format for many years. It has brought much fruit from the petitions I have laid before His throne.

Another way to organize our times of prayer is to pray according to our relationships with those for whom we are praying. We can pray first for immediate and then extended family members. Then, we can go to God on behalf of friends, co-workers, fellow students, teammates, ministry partners, acquaintances, strangers, and enemies. Let me explain.

First, our prayers can involve immediate and extended family. In Colossians 3:19-21, Paul commands, "Husbands, love your wives, and do not be bitter against them. Children, obey your parents in all things, for this [obedience] pleases the Lord. Fathers, don't provoke your children, so that they won't be discouraged." One way in which we can love them is to pray for them. In Ephesians 5:25, He uses Christ as our example of love, "Husbands, love your wives, even as Christ also loved the assembly, and gave himself up for it." We know from our previous study, Christ often prayed for those who were His disciples. We are to do the same for our own immediate and extended families.

Second, we could pray for our friends. In John 15:14, the Lord called His disciples His friends. He states, "You are my friends, if you do whatever I command you." They did and they were. As He prayed for His disciples, He prayed for His friends. Then, we ought also to pray for our friends as well.

Third, we could pray for those who are partners in our ministries. In 2 Timothy 1:3, Paul tells Timothy, his fellow minister, "I thank God, whom I serve as my forefathers did, with a pure conscience. How unceasing is my memory of you in my petitions, night and day." The apostle brought his partner in service to the Lord before God's throne regularly.

Fourth, we could pray for those to whom we minister. In Colossians 1:3, Paul opens with, "We give thanks to God the Father of our Lord Jesus Christ, praying always for you." In 1

Thessalonians 1:2, Paul again says that he is praying for those he is serving in the gospel, "We always give thanks to God for all of you, mentioning you in our prayers." So, we should pray for those we are serving the Lord individually by name or even as a group.

Fifth, we could pray for our neighbors. In Galatians 5:14, Paul explains this principle, "For the whole law is fulfilled in one word, in this: 'You shall love your neighbor as yourself.'" Would not prayer be a powerful way to love our neighbors? This term "neighbors" refers to everyone besides ourselves, which includes those at work, school, in our neighborhoods, at the places we regularly frequent, on our teams, in our clubs, and even strangers and enemies. In Romans 1:9, the apostle prays for the Roman church even though He had not planted it or visited it yet. He writes, "For God is my witness, whom I serve in my spirit in the Good News of his Son, how unceasingly I make mention of you always in my prayers."

In Romans 9:2-3, the apostle told the Romans how much he desired the Jews to come to Christ. He described it this way, "That I have great sorrow and unceasing pain in my heart. For I could wish that I myself were accursed from Christ for my brothers' [all] sake, my relatives according to the flesh." Therefore, we can include our acquaintances or strangers in our many prayers. Who else will pray for them, if not us? Can anyone ever have enough people sending up prayers for them?

So, what would our prayer request include? First, we must pray for their salvation if any are unsaved. In 1 Timothy 2:1-2, Paul commands this very thing, "I exhort therefore, first of all, that petitions, prayers, intercessions, and thanksgivings, be made for all men: for kings and all who are in high places; that we may lead a tranquil and quiet life in all godliness and reverence. For this is good and acceptable in the sight of God our Savior; who desires all people to be saved and come to full knowledge of the truth" (DEJ) The Lord God desires all men to be saved and prayers are definitely a part of this.

Second, our requests for ourselves and other Christians for whom we are praying may include anything that concerns us. In Philippians 4:6, Paul writes, "In nothing be anxious, but in everything, by prayer and petition with thanksgiving, let your requests be made known to God." One can do a simple concordance study on the word "pray" and many different topics for prayer will come up.

A method that has worked well is praying according to the names of people. I start with my family and begin my prayer with, "Father, I pray for (insert name)..." Then, I will make a specific request or ask the Lord to bless them in a way that glorifies Him. I prefer this way because it allows me to know that I have included in my prayers the people I love the most. So, when obstacles come our way, we can deal with them through prayer. As God works in our hearts and the situations that we face, we should experience less and less emptiness, fear, pain, regret, guilt, desperation, despair, aimlessness, anxiety, and uncertainty. Instead, we certainly will see an increase in peace, calm, joy, faith, comfort, hope, love, grace, courage, purpose, and trust.

Chapter 5

Seek Your Personal Holiness

The living of the Christian life in a righteous manner is an important key to not only pleasing our Lord Jesus but also to filling our souls with calm, peace, joy, faith, comfort, hope, love, grace, courage, purpose, and trust. As we seek personal holiness, our bound and captive hearts will be released from the chains of fear, emptiness, pain, regret, desperation, guilt, despair, broken hearts, anxiety, worry, financial uncertainty, and a lack of purpose that we might be experiencing.

Often, we put ourselves into bondage or at least we can compound the bondage we may feel because we aren't living according to the instruction manual laid out by our maker. He knows the best way to live, and we must follow it. When we do, we can free ourselves from our self-imposed or self-encumbered captivity. God's blueprint for the way we ought to live as Christians involves three areas: godliness, holiness, and righteousness. These should be expressed in thoughts, words, actions, and attitudes. As we think, speak, behave, and value God's ways rather than man's, we will truly find the relief we are looking for.

When we received Christ as Savior and Lord, we became brand new creations. In 2 Corinthians 5:17, Paul describes it, "Therefore if anyone is in Christ, he is a new creation. The old things have passed away. Behold, all things have become new." The word "new" means "brand new, new of a different kind." Our old inner person and ways of thinking, feeling, and doing became brand new. Then, we begin the important transformation process (sanctification) which will mature us into godly people who measure up to Christ's stature.

These three truths can be found in Paul's exhortation in his letter to the Ephesians. In chapter four, verse twenty-four, he writes the following, "And put on the new man, who in the likeness of God has been created in righteousness and holiness of truth." Here, Paul encourages Christians to behave like brand new people who act godly (in likeness of God), holy, and righteous. The Greek word translated "put on" carries the idea of "putting on clothing." We are to put on the new man by putting on the thoughts, words, deeds, and attitudes of godliness, holiness, and righteousness.

Though these three important words seem to conjure up in our minds the same ideas, they are all very different. We will begin with the concept of "holiness." The Greek word translated "holiness" refers to being "set apart" or "separate from." We as Christians are completely set apart for God. We are to be separate from the world. We are "wholly different" in our thoughts, words, actions, attitudes, and values. People will say about us, "There is something different about them. They don't think, speak, and act like us."

In 1 Peter 1:15-16, the apostle Peter makes this assertion, "But just as he who called you is holy, you yourselves also be holy in all of your behavior; because it is written, 'You shall be holy; for I am holy.'" As believers, we must have lives "set apart" onto God. In the second chapter, Peter describes this calling. In verse nine, he declares, "But you are a chosen race, a royal priesthood, a holy nation, a people for God's own possession, that you may proclaim the excellence of him who called you out of darkness into his marvelous light."

So, we have been set apart to God and separated from the world to become wholly different royal priests, a nation, and a people that God possesses as His own. As priests we are to offer spiritual sacrifices. What does this mean? Paul uses the same kind of descriptive language to speak of the offering of our bodies in service to Christ. In Romans 12:1, he wrote this, "Therefore I urge you, brothers, by the mercies of God, to present your bodies [every part] a living sacrifice, holy, acceptable to God, which is your spiritual service." And just like His Old Testament priests made sacrifices of animals on an altar, we are to offer our bodies (mind, lips, hands, feet, and heart) to God in service. We should offer to Him every day all that we are.

In 2 Peter 3:11, Peter calls this "holy living." He says, "Therefore since all these things will be destroyed like this, what kind of people ought you to be in holy living and godliness." We are to live wholly different from those who are not God's own possession. To do this, we must grow in our holiness. In Ephesians 2:21, Paul utilizes the analogy of the church being a building that is growing into a holy temple, "in whom the whole building, fitted together, grows into a holy temple in the Lord." As we practice the spiritual growth principles in the Holy Scriptures, we will grow in our holiness becoming more and more wholly different.

The second truth is that we are to think, speak, and act in a right manner. We are to live righteously. This is directly opposed to living in an unrighteous or wrong manner. Who decides what is right and wrong? Who decides whether my thoughts, words, actions, or values are right or wrong? The answer is God. If God says that it is right, then it is right. If God says that it is wrong, then it is wrong. Period.

All over the Bible, God is called "righteous." In Psalm 11:7, the Psalmist cries, "For Yahweh {God] is righteous. He loves righteousness. The upright shall see his face." Then, in Psalm 71:19, it says, "Your righteousness also, God, reaches to the heavens; you have done great things. God, who is like you?" God is above all and whatever He thinks, speaks, and acts is always "right." This right way is in the Bible.

A characteristic of all Christians is righteousness or right living according to God. The apostle John teaches this very truth in his first letter. In 1 John 2:29, he writes, "If you know that he [God] is righteous, you know that everyone who practices righteousness has been born of him." Then he contrasts those believers with those who do not believe. In 1 John 3:10, John makes this distinction, "In this the children of God are revealed, and the children of the devil. Whoever doesn't do [practice] righteousness is not of God, neither is he who doesn't love his brother."

So, how do we actually do this? As mentioned above, we must present our bodies as living sacrifices every day. In Romans 6:19, Paul clarifies, "I speak in human terms because of the weakness of your flesh, for as you presented your members as servants to uncleanness and to wickedness upon wickedness, even so now present your members as servants to righteousness for sanctification." We must learn that we cannot present ourselves before sin to serve our lusts and desires; but instead, we present ourselves to righteousness to serve His wants and desires.

Since we have a heavenly Father who loves us, we can be assured that He will help us along this path by disciplining us if we stray from His righteous path. In Hebrews 12:7-8, the author explains, "It is for discipline that you endure. God deals with you as with children, for what son is there whom his father doesn't discipline [train]? But if you [those who call themselves Christians] are without discipline, of which all have been made partakers, then are you illegitimate, and not children." The Greek word translated "discipline" refers to discipline in training rather than punishment in judgment. In verse 11, the author says, "All chastening seems for the present to be not joyous but grievous; yet afterward it yields the peaceful fruit of righteousness to those who have been exercised thereby. Notice, he calls it "peaceful fruit." If we are willing to live righteously, it produces all kinds of fruit that is peaceful. Will this not bring the relief that we seek?

In 2 Timothy 2:22, Paul writes to Timothy, his younger missionary companion, "Flee from youthful lusts; but pursue righteousness, faith, love, and peace with those who call on the Lord out of a pure heart." We must be pursuing after the righteous way of God and not the unrighteous way that comes out of lustful desires and perceived needs.

The third term is the Greek word which is translated "godly." This conveys the idea of thinking, speaking, doing, and valuing "religious or spiritual" things. This concept is different than righteousness (general good behavior) and holiness (being separate from the sinning of the world). It comes from two Greek words meaning "good worship or well-done reverence." It refers to being "reverent" by the thinking, speaking, doing, and valuing of spiritual things which demonstrate a deep respect for and honor of the God. Some of these involve reading the Scriptures, praying, attending church services, fellowshipping with the saints, the taking of communion regularly, and meeting the needs of others.

This meaning can be seen clearly in its use as an adjective by Luke to describe Cornelius. In Acts 10:2, Luke writes, "A devout man, and one who feared God with all his house, who gave gifts for the needy generously to the people, and always prayed to God." Here, we see elements of his "fear of God (reverence)," which he displayed by his generous giving to the needy and his many prayers. Because of Cornelius's devotion to God, it was determined that he would receive the gift of the Holy Spirit by Peter to demonstrate that God had brought the gospel to the Gentiles as He did the Jews. So, the Lord God told Cornelius to send his friends to Peter to request that Peter come and stay in his home.

In Acts 10:22, Luke records the arrival of the friends and how they described Cornelius to the apostle, "They said, 'Cornelius, a centurion, a righteous man and one who fears God, and well-spoken of by all the nation of the Jews, was directed by a holy angel to invite you to his house, and to listen to what you say.'" He was a righteous (did many good deeds and obeyed God's commandments) man. He was a fair and decent commander in the Roman army because the man was well-spoken of by all that knew him.

When Peter arrived, Cornelius humbled himself before the apostle and explained what God had done. In Acts 10:30, Luke pens, "Cornelius said, 'Four days ago, I was fasting until this hour, and at the ninth hour, I prayed in my house, and behold, a man stood before me in bright clothing [angel], and said, "Cornelius, your prayer is heard, and your gifts to the needy are remembered in the sight of God. Send therefore to Joppa, and summon Simon, who is also called Peter. He lodges in the house of a tanner named Simon, by the seaside. When he comes, he will speak to you."'"

Cornelius was fasting and praying and giving. These are all the actions of a reverent, devout man. Here Cornelius was a God-fearing Jew and the Jews respected him for his devotion to their God. When we demonstrate this same kind of godliness (reverence for the Lord), which is produced from godly thoughts and values and springs forth into godly words and actions, we put God on display in our lives. in these things, we demonstrate that we are His.

What are the "religious, devout things of the Lord that we should be participating in? In Acts 2:42, Luke describes the devout practices of the early Christians, "They continued steadfastly in the apostles' teaching and fellowship, in the breaking of bread, and prayer." Believers devote themselves to the Scriptures, prayer, fellowship (partnership activities to grow the kingdom), and communion. Then in verses 44-45, Luke continues, "All who believed were together, and had all things in common. They sold their possessions and goods, and distributed them to all, according as anyone had need." These devout people were generously meeting each other's physical needs as well as spiritual. Here, they had to hold all things they owned in common because so many came to the Lord Jesus, who were Jewish, and would have been disowned by their families.

Then, Luke concludes with this description in verses 46-47, " Day by day, continuing steadfastly with one accord in the temple, and breaking bread at home, they took their food with gladness and singleness of heart, praising God, and having favor with all the people. The Lord added to the assembly day by day those who were being saved." Notice, there were gatherings of Christians daily in both the temple and house to house. They ate together, praised God together, and were single-minded of heart. The point is simple: to be devout is to participate in the righteous, holy things that those who believe in Christ do. Just as there are thoughts, words, actions, attitudes, and values that guide the behavior in any group of people, Christianity has their own. These are the ones that we, as believers, who are "devout" engage in individually and with others.

These three characteristics of Christian living are centered on one beautiful principle: we love Christ by obeying Him. This life is essentially a life of obedience. This is the teaching of our Lord and Savior. In John 14:15, Jesus declared, "If you love me, keep my commandments." Then in verse 21, Christ added, "One who has my commandments, and keeps them, that person is one who loves me. One who loves me will be loved by my Father, and I will love him, and will reveal myself to him." Then in verses 23-24, the Lord proclaimed, "If a man loves me, he will keep my word. My Father will love him, and we will come to him, and make our home with him. He who doesn't love me doesn't keep my words. The word which you hear isn't mine, but the Father's who sent me." In John 15:10, Jesus continued, "If you keep my commandments, you will remain in my love; even as I have kept my Father's commandments and remain in his love."

These statements need no explanation but are very clear. We are to demonstrate our love for Christ by letting that love pour forth into obedience. Our wholly different, right living in a devout manner has much to do with keeping the commandments and following God's ways laid out in the Bible. The Bible tells us how God, His Son, and His Spirit think, speak, act and what they value. To measure up to the stature of Christ we must get to know the Word and then obey it. In James 1:22, the inspired writer penned, "But be doers of the word, and not only hearers, deluding your own selves." We must do the Word. How can we accomplish this?

In order to live a holy, righteous, and devout life in true obedience to the Lord, we must embrace this new manner of living with our whole hearts. In Proverbs 15:9, wise King Solomon wrote, "The way of the wicked is an abomination to Yahweh, but he loves him who follows after righteousness." This word translated "follow" means to "pursue, run after, or chase." It does not denote casual following but a determined action of the will and body.

In Genesis 14:14, the word is used to describe Abraham's pursuit of his nephew's captors. It says, "When Abram heard that his relative was taken captive, he led out his trained men, born in his house, three hundred and eighteen, and pursued as far as Dan." In Exodus 14:8, it was utilized by Moses to portray the determined actions of the Pharaoh to chase and destroy God's people, Israel, after they had departed from Egypt. He writes, "Yahweh [God] hardened the heart of

Pharaoh king of Egypt, and he pursued the children of Israel; for the children of Israel went out with a high hand."

We need to have this kind of determination in our pursuit after obedience to the Lord. In 2 Timothy 2:22, Paul gives a similar exhortation. Here, he is writing to Timothy, a young pastor and explains how to live life before the congregation, "Flee from youthful lusts; but pursue righteousness, faith, love, and peace with those who call on the Lord out of a pure heart." This Greek word means "to make to run or flee, put to flight, or drive away." In 1 Corinthians 15:9, Paul uses it to describe how he pursued Christians to harm them, "For I am the least of the apostles, who is not worthy to be called an apostle, because I persecuted the assembly of God." The vigor that Paul had in his pursuit after the persecution of Christians before becoming a Christian was the determined action he wanted Timothy to have in his pursuit after right behavior among other things.

Exactly how do we "pursue" righteousness, holiness, and a devout way of life? It can be accomplished by standing at the throne of God and offering our bodies (thoughts, words, actions, attitudes, and values) as living sacrifices. In Romans 12:1-2, Paul writes, "Therefore I urge you, brothers, by the mercies of God, to present your bodies a living sacrifice, holy, acceptable to God, which is your spiritual service." We must not be conformed to this world but be transformed by the renewing of our minds. This is accomplished, as we have already seen, through the reading, studying, and applying of God's Word. Then, we must come before the Lord and offer Him ourselves as holy instruments in service to Him. This process leads to living holy lives pleasing to Him.

Another way we can live a holy, righteous, and devout life is to avoid the unrighteous ways of our old lives. This does not mean that we should cut ourselves off from people but to keep ourselves removed from whatever evil we may have been involved in. We should heed the words of Peter in 1 Peter 1:14 when he described our new lives in Christ, "As children of obedience, not conforming yourselves according to your former lusts as in your ignorance." He explains that before knowing Christ, we were ignorant of the evil we were doing. Obedience means we should not behave as formerly.

In chapter 4:2-3, he continues to say, "That you no longer should live the rest of your time in the flesh for the lusts of men, but for the will of God. For we have spent enough of our past time doing the desire of the Gentiles, and having walked in lewdness, lusts, drunken binges, orgies, carousings, and abominable idolatries." This kind of living away from God can spark, ignite, or instigate the kinds of negative issues we are facing. If we desire release from these chains of despair, emptiness, pain, regret, desperation, guilt, anxiety, worry, broken hearts, fear, uncertainty, or the lack of purpose that we might be experiencing, then we should reject our old ways (life) without Christ. This will greatly help. A life of obedience will provide the calm, peace, joy, faith, comfort, hope, love, grace, courage, purpose, or trust we might seek. As we pursue personal holiness, our bound and captive hearts will find release and real healing.

A third way that might aid us, as believers, in our pursuit after righteous, holy, and devout living is the handling of our companions from our old lives. These are the ones that have not received Christ who are still living in our old ways. First, we could consider avoiding a friend or family member if the temptation is too great to sin with the person. Our holiness must take precedence. In Proverbs 4:14-15, Solomon states this, "Don't enter into the path of the wicked. Don't walk in the way of evil men. Avoid it, and don't pass by it. Turn from it and pass on." In 1 Corinthians 15:33, Paul says this, "Don't be deceived! "Evil companionships corrupt good morals."

Another approach we might take is to change our roles in our relationships from being a companion of wickedness with them to a companion of salt and light. In Matthew 5:13-16, Jesus spoke of this kind of companionship, "You are the salt of the earth, but if the salt has lost its flavor, with what will it be salted? It is then good for nothing, but to be cast out and trodden under the feet of men. You are the light of the world. A city located on a hill can't be hidden. Neither do you light a lamp, and put it under a measuring basket, but on a stand; and it shines to all who are in the house. Even so, let your light shine before men; that they may see your good works, and glorify your Father who is in heaven."

The salt in ancient times was utilized for the preservation of food and then its seasoning. In Mark 9:50, Jesus speaks of salt's ability to flavor foods, "Salt is good, but if the salt has lost its saltiness, with what will you season it? Have salt in yourselves, and be at peace with one another." In Luke 14:34, the Lord refers to this same concept, "Salt is good, but if the salt becomes flat and tasteless, with what do you season it?" What are we to season or flavor our relationships with? We provide the good news as its flavor. In Colossians 4:6, Paul encourages the believers to season their speech like salt, "Let your speech always be with grace, seasoned with salt, that you may know how you ought to answer each one." Here, he is discussing the sharing of the gospel. We should be walking and talking the gospel with our friends. We know that they need the Lord.

Light refers to both moral and intellectual truth. When we think, speak, and act in moral righteousness and in biblical truth, we put our lights on a hill. When we live in moral wickedness and falsehoods against the Bible, we cover our lights and bring darkness. So, we need to be salt and light in all our relationships. If this is not possible, because we are too tempted to sin with them, we must avoid them.

The living of the Christian life in a righteous manner not only pleases our Lord Jesus but also fills our souls with calm, peace, gladness, faith, comfort, hope, love, grace, courage, purpose, and trust. If we seek personal holiness in our lives, our bound and captive hearts should be released from the chains of our fear, emptiness, pain, regret, desperation, guilt, despair, anxiety, broken hearts, a lack of purpose, and the uncertainty that we might be experiencing. We can remove the spiritual bondage we possess through holy living.

Chapter 6

Fellowship with Steady Interaction

As we continue in our journey of discovery concerning the important essentials of the Christian life, we now come to our interaction with the saints of God in His church. We must fellowship with the saints in steady interaction. This can bring much relief from our chains and produce the calm, peace, joy, faith, comfort, hope, love, grace, courage, trust, and purpose for which we are searching. Ministering to our brothers and sisters in Christ and accepting their ministry is critical in releasing us from the bondage of our emptiness, fear of death, tormented and pain-filled bodies, desperation facing tragedy, regret for past actions, guilt for past sins, deep despair, broken hearts, anxiety, and worry, financial uncertainty, and lack of purpose.

The biblical word for this interaction is "fellowship." In 1 John 1:6-7, he speaks of our "fellowship" with one another. The word connotes a "joint participation or partnership" in something. We are involved in a joint participation in the advancement of the Kingdom of God both numerically and spiritually. We partner with others to share the gospel and mature the saints. This primarily refers not to what we can get from others but what we can give to others. Much relief can come by taking our minds off of ourselves and placing them on others as we serve them. This is not friendship.

We will discuss advancing the kingdom in the chapter on sharing the gospel regularly. We can fellowship together as we share the gospel. In this chapter, we will deal with our fellowship with other believers to provoke them to grow in Christ. This may involve both the meeting of spiritual needs and also physical needs. The Christian life was never meant to be lived as a group of individuals in a kingdom; instead, we work together for the common goal of glorifying Christ in all we do. We focus on others in our fellowship as others focus on us. We are to provoke each other to become mature.

In Hebrews 10:24-25, the author of the book entreats the individual saints in the church to continue attending the local assembly. Why? He explains, "Let us consider how to provoke one another to love and good works, not forsaking our own assembling together, as the custom of some is, but exhorting one another; and so much the more, as you see the Day approaching." We are to be meeting with one another regularly not for the sake of ourselves but for what we can do in the lives of others.

The Greek word translated "provoke" means "to sharpen, stimulate, or provoke." The root of the word is used in Acts 17:16 when Luke wrote, "Now while Paul waited for them at Athens, his spirit was provoked within him as he saw the city full of idols." Paul entered the city, and he saw idols everywhere. This stimulated [provoked] him to take a stand with the gospel. We are to stimulate other Christians to live lives pleasing to God.

The word translated "forsake" means "to desert, leave in straits, leave helpless, or abandon." It refers to a complete and total abandonment of someone to survive on their own. In Matthew 27:46, the word is used by Jesus when He was abandoned by the Father as He was punished for our sins, "About the ninth hour Jesus cried with a loud voice, saying, 'Eli, Eli, lima sabachthani?' That is, 'My God, my God, why have you forsaken me?'" The implication is clear. When we do not attend the gatherings of believers, we have forsaken and abandoned them. We have left them to spiritually fend for themselves. Why? They need us. Notice, the emphasis is not on the meeting of our needs but on the needs of others.

Then, the author says that we are to be "exhorting" one another. The word translated "exhorting" means "to come alongside." It carries the idea of someone coming alongside another and comforting, encouraging, and helping them. A Christian who may be struggling with similar kinds of issues need to be encouraged also. As we learn how to find release from our emotional and physical captivity, we should show one another how to do it. When our minds are fully focused on someone else, we will not get stuck in our own issues which lead to discouragement and hopelessness. Of course, as a general word, it refers to all issues of the Christian life.

Now, what does this "fellowship" look like? How do we provoke one another to love and good deeds? The answer is best found in what is called the biblical "one anothers." In the New Testament, the writers exhort Christians to fellowship with one another using these two words. We are encouraged to love and honor one another (Romans 12:10), build up one another in the faith (Romans 14:19;), bear the burdens of one another (Galatians 6:2), forgive one another (Ephesians 4:32), teach and warn one another (Colossians 3:16), comfort one another (1 Thessalonians 4:18-19), serve one another (1 Peter 4:10), exhort one another (1 Thessalonians 5:11), and pray for one another (James 5:16). This is just a few of the numerous descriptions of fellowship together. Notice, these involve persistent interaction. This steady fellowship with others in Jesus Christ should involve spontaneous participation and structured partnership. This should mean more than just the attendance at a local worship service. If our hearts are open, at times the Lord will create an opportunity to fellowship. At other times, Christians should make opportunities to serve and minister.

The fellowship of the church involves practicing the "one anothers" whenever we are around Christians. Though this can be done casually before and after a worship service, it is best accomplished in our daily living. When the author of Hebrews spoke of the "assembling together," he didn't mean just the worship service but all kinds of gatherings among the saints. In Acts 2:42, Luke describes the daily interaction of believers, "They continued steadfastly in the apostles' teaching and fellowship, in the breaking of bread [the Lord's Table], and prayer." Then in verse 46, he adds, "Day by day, continuing steadfastly with one accord in the temple, and breaking bread at home, they took their food with gladness and singleness of heart." Then in Acts 5:42, he writes, "Every day, in the temple and at home, they never stopped teaching and preaching Jesus, the Christ." The saints were gathering formally and informally in the temple and in their homes.

Our spontaneous participation involves spending time together. We can enjoy activities together, invite people into our homes, and participate in hobbies or sports with one another. Now, this is not the fellowship part, but it develops relationships that could become fellowship when we partner together. This happens when we practice the "one anothers" to each other or other believers, minister and serve the saints together, and join together in sharing the good news to the unsaved. To practice this spontaneous fellowship, we do not need to be close friends with believers. We need only see a spiritual or physical need and meet it together.

Our fellowship in a structured partnership involves the many organized gatherings of the church. We should attend the worship services and join bible study, prayer, or service groups. Here, we are able to regularly interact with people, meet their spiritual and physical needs, and allow the other believers to do the same for us. Here is a key to the release from the captivity we feel. We must allow others into our lives, so they might minister to us. We should not face our trials alone. God desires to extend His love, grace, mercy, strength, and power through others toward us.

We cannot rely solely on professionals to walk with us on our journeys. There will be others who have not walked in our shoes but can empathize and sympathize with us. There will be others who have walked down the road we walk or a similar path and will be able to comfort us. In 2 Corinthians 1:3-4, Paul explains this, "Blessed be the God and Father of our Lord Jesus Christ, the Father of mercies and God of all comfort, who comforts us in all our affliction so that we will be able to comfort those who are in any affliction with the comfort with which we ourselves are comforted by God." He was able to comfort others because he also had experienced God's comfort. How can believers minister to others and allow others to minister to us?

In order to participate in this deeply spiritual endeavor, we must prepare our hearts. We do this by reading the word and praying to wisdom. This will fill us with the fruits of the Spirit. The fruits of the Spirit are the very foundation of fellowshipping together. In Galatians 5:22-23, Paul describes the essential fruits we must have in our hearts, "But the fruit of the Spirit is love, joy, peace, patience, kindness, goodness, faith, gentleness, and self-control." If we are controlled by these fruits, then our hearts will be ready. How do we find this "filling?" In Ephesians 5:19, Paul says that the filling of the Spirit will produce "speaking to one another in psalms, hymns, and spiritual songs; singing, and making melody in your heart to the Lord. In Colossians 3:6, he describes the very same results from the reading of the Word; Christians will be "teaching and admonishing one another with psalms, hymns, and spiritual songs, singing with grace in your heart to the Lord." Spending time in God's Word will fill us with the Spirit. This "filling" simply means to be controlled by the Holy Spirit at any given moment.

As we read the Scriptures in preparation for ministering to others and allowing others to minister to us, we should pray for wisdom. We need the wisdom of God to know what to say and do for people. In James 1:5, he encourages, "But if any of you lacks wisdom, let him ask of God, who gives to all liberally and without reproach; and it will be given to him." Then in James 3:13, the inspired writer declares this, "Who is wise and understanding among you? Let him show by his good conduct that his deeds are done in gentleness of wisdom." In James 3:17, he describes this wisdom's origin and characteristics, "But the wisdom that is from above is first pure, then peaceful, gentle, reasonable, full of mercy and good fruits, without partiality, and without hypocrisy." We can see how important it is to meet spiritual needs by the peaceful, gentle, reasonable, merciful, impartial words that come out of love, joy, peace, patience, kindness, goodness, gentleness, and faith in our hearts.

Another way is to really listen. As God's people share with us, we need to listen intently. Sometimes, we get so caught up in what we want to say that we do not hear the person to whom we desire to minister. Careful listening provides an opportunity to share in the joys, sorrows, and difficulties of other believers. We can praise God for their joys and pray or provide support for their numerous sorrows and problems. In 1 Thessalonians 3:6, Paul explains to the church the news he had heard about them from Timothy, "But when Timothy came just now to us from you, and brought us glad news of your faith and love, and that you have good memories of us always, longing to see us, even as we also long to see you." These words convey Paul's desire to know how they were and what they were experiencing. We should do the same as we attempt to provoke others to love and good deeds.

While we listen, it should be with a real openness. Not all believers are at the same level in their spiritual maturity. It is important that we really respect believers as they share their burdens. Paul explains this principle in 1 Corinthians 8:1. He writes, "Now concerning things sacrificed to idols: We know that we all have knowledge. Knowledge puffs up, but love builds up." Here, the apostle is not saying we should not be knowledgeable in the Scriptures, of course we should. The Bible is what helps us grow as Christians. He is describing believers who look down upon and are impatient with the struggles of the saints. Instead, we must always be building the saints up in our love. This means loving tolerance as we minister to them. We may put much time into ministering to them, and they may fall several times, so we should show patience while supporting them.

How can we gain support from others? Believers should be willing to share our difficulties with others. This should be done with common sense. We must realize that others need to know our struggles to support us. Though Paul did not share specific sins in detail with the members of his churches, the apostle certainly shared his general struggles. In Romans 7:14-20, he says, "For we know that the law is spiritual, but I am fleshly, sold under sin. For I don't know what I am doing. For I don't practice what I desire to do; but what I hate, that I do. But if what I don't desire, that I do, I consent to the law that it is good. So now it is no more I that do it, but sin...dwells in me. For I know that in me, that is, in my flesh, dwells no good thing. For desire is present with me, but I don't find it doing that which is good. For the good which I desire, I don't do; but the evil which I don't desire, that I practice. But if what I don't desire, that I do, it is no more I that do it, but sin which dwells in me." As we can see, Paul shared his challenges with us, so we ought to share ours with others.

In 2 Corinthians 1:8, he described the despair of life that he felt when the persecutions became too intense. He shared his feelings, "We don't desire to have you uninformed, brothers, concerning our affliction which happened to us in Asia, that we were weighed down exceedingly, beyond our power, so much that we despaired even of life." If we do the same, then we can receive the support we need to be released from our captivity. If we are willing to open up with others about our bondage, this will allow them to have an impact on us.

As we have now seen, our journey of the Christian life must involve interaction with the saints of God in His local church. When we, as believers, fellowship with Christians by ministering to them and allowing them to minister to us in steady interaction, we should find much relief from our chains and possess the calm, peace, joy, faith, comfort, hope, love, grace, courage, purpose, and trust that we seek.

Chapter 7

Share the Gospel Regularly

Another aspect of living the Christian life that aids in our maturity in Jesus Christ is sharing the gospel with others. Being used by God to bring someone into the kingdom is not only an incredible experience but allows us to take our eyes off ourselves and put them on others. It stimulates us to read the Bible and pray more often. As we support them, we will also grow in Christ. Why? Sharing the gospel will challenge us to vibrantly follow the many steps of growth ourselves. Lastly, it brings tremendous joy. As a result, we can find our release from captivity. This can produce calm, peace, faith, comfort, hope, love, grace, courage, purpose, and trust.

Jesus has given kingdom people the task of sharing the gospel and bringing others into the kingdom. He Himself was the light. The apostle John opens his gospel with this important truth. In John 1:4-5, John describes the light of the Lord Jesus, "In him was life, and the life was the light of men. The light shines in the darkness, and...hasn't overcome it."

The word translated "light" has two aspects to it. The first is doctrinal. Here the light of spiritual truth is contrasted with the darkness of spiritual error. The second aspect is moral and contrasts the light of righteousness and holiness with the darkness of sin, evil, and wickedness. So, John is saying that Christ came to reveal in Himself what truth and righteousness is in the midst of a world filled with lies and wickedness. This is what Jesus Himself claimed. In John 12:46, He declared, "I have come as a light into the world, that whoever believes in me may not remain in darkness."

This is the true gospel uttered in the simplest of terms. This light is the truth of who God is. It reveals that Christ had come to die for mankind and people must receive Him as Savior and Lord. Why? The Lord God is righteous, and man simply is not. Man lives in the darkness of thinking that he can find God, deny God, or create a god on his own. He is basically good, and all things will work out in the end. Jesus came to explain that this was not the case at all; instead, judgment for sin will damn all mankind forever and ever.

Man must take on the righteousness of Christ by grace through faith. In Ephesians 2, the apostle Paul described the saving good news in this way. In verses 4-5, he stated, "But God, being rich in mercy, for his great love with which he loved us, even when we were dead through our trespasses, made us alive together with Christ (by grace you have been saved)." How is this accomplished? In verses 8-9, the apostle explained, "For by grace you have been saved through faith, and that not of yourselves; it is the gift of God, not of works, that no one would boast." God's grace is poured out upon man in his sin as a gift received by faith. Then, Paul adds the purpose for which we have been saved. Receiving Christ is not the end but the beginning of our time on earth.

Then what is our purpose while dwelling on this planet? It is to do good works. In verse 10, he pens, "For we are his workmanship, created in Christ Jesus for good works, which God prepared before [the beginning of the world] that we would walk in them." This is not just any old "good works" we choose but specific thoughts, words, and actions that honor God. These are based on His commandments in the Scriptures. One of His commandments is to share this good news with others; that is, we are to be lights to the world.

This is why the Lord Jesus told His disciples and thereby all generations of Christians that they too are lights unto the dark world. In Matthew 5:14-15, the Lord proclaimed to His disciples, "You are the light of the world. A city located on a hill can't be hidden. Neither do you light a lamp, and put it under a measuring basket, but on a stand; and it shines to all who are in the house." Jesus is saying that we must shine our lights as lamps and never cover them over. We should never hide what we believe and who we are in Christ individually. Also, as a city of saints, we must be on top of a hill shining our lights in the same way as a church.

So, we should shine our lights as Christians individually and together. There are two ways in which we personally shine our lights to the world by living a righteous life before all and then verbally sharing the good news.

First, all true Christians are to shine their lights by living righteously before the world. The sharing of the good news is the truth displayed rather than error and living in a holy way is the righteousness displayed rather than wickedness. In Matthew 5:16, the Lord explained that to shine their lights Christians must also live righteous lives. He says, "Even so, let your light shine before men; that they may see your good works, and glorify your Father who is in heaven."

In Philippians 2:14-15, the apostle declared that the saints were to appear as lights in the world. This meant that they were to live righteously before the world. Paul wrote these powerful words, "Do all things without murmurings and disputes, that you may become blameless [no fault found] and harmless [pure], children of God without blemish in the midst of a crooked [wicked] and perverse [opposed to God] generation, among whom you [believers] are seen as lights in the world."

We, as believers, are to be lights in our evil, dark world. We should live in harmony, without disputes or grumbling, and with holy habits. This should be seen as shining our lights in the midst of people living in the darkness of sin and opposition to God. Paul discusses this same concept again in his letter to the Ephesians using the same terms of light and darkness again. In Ephesians 5:8, Paul explains, "For you were once darkness, but are now light in the Lord. Walk as children of light." We must walk (meaning walk about living our lives) as children of light. Our words and actions must be the words and actions of those in the light. We must be steadfast in righteousness.

In Colossians 2:6, Paul commands those in the church to walk (live their lives) in a manner worthy of the Lord. Paul writes, "Therefore as you have received Christ Jesus the Lord, so walk in Him." Paul also states that they were to live to please Him in every area of their lives (in all respects). In Ephesians 4:1, the apostle entreats his readers to live for the Lord Jesus Christ. He writes, "I therefore, the prisoner in the Lord, beg you to walk worthily of the calling with which you were called." We were called out of the temporal world into eternal life. We came out of the darkness and should walk worthy of that holy calling. Again, Paul was in prison waiting for his trial because the apostle walked worthy. In 1 Thessalonians 2:12, Paul instructs the new believers to live worthy of God, the Father, when he writes, "To the end that you should walk worthily of God, who calls you into his own Kingdom and glory."

We are members of the kingdom and recipients of His glory manifested in His blessings. We must always walk worthy of this great honor. This is not the earning of our salvation but simply the display of it. In 1 Thessalonians 4:1, Paul adds these powerful words, "Finally then, brothers, we beg...you in the Lord Jesus, that as you received...how you ought to walk and to please God, that you abound more and more." Their goal was to grow more and more righteous.

In the letter of 1 John 1:7-9, the beloved disciple John calls this "walking in the light." This righteous lifestyle is a great testimony of the Lord Jesus Christ. He writes, "But if we walk in the light, as he [Christ} is in the light, we have fellowship with one another, and the blood of Jesus Christ, his Son, cleanses us from all sin. If we say that we have no sin, we deceive ourselves, and the truth is not in us. If we confess our sins, he is faithful and righteous to forgive us the sins, and to cleanse us from all unrighteousness."

As we walk in the light by living righteous lives before the world, we evidence the fact that the blood of Jesus is cleansing us from our sins. Here John implies a pattern: we walk in the light, we stumble, we confess, we are forgiven, and then we continue to walk.

Second, we should share the gospel as we live righteously before the world. In Philippians 2:16, speaking of our lights, the apostle writes, "Holding up the word of life, that I may have something to boast in the day of Christ, that I didn't run in vain nor labor in vain." The Lord passed His light shining ministry to His twelve disciples and through them to us. In Matthew 10:27, He commanded this, "What I tell you in the darkness, speak in the light; and what you hear whispered in the ear, proclaim on the housetops."

They were to share the truth (His light) with others (their lights). When Paul entered Pisidian Antioch to preach the gospel, he told them that he had this very mission. In Acts 13:47, he says, "For so has the Lord commanded us, saying, 'I have set you as a light for the Gentiles, that you should bring salvation to the uttermost parts of the earth.'" The apostle saw himself as a light shining into their dark city of error and sin. The Lord could have selected a variety of ways in which He could have revealed His gospel to the world, but He chose us to proclaim it as lights in the darkness.

How is this accomplished? In Romans 10:14, the apostle Paul provides an answer in a series of rhetorical questions. In Romans 10:14-15, he writes, "How then will they [those in darkness] call on him in whom they have not believed? How will they believe in him whom they have not heard? How will they hear [the gospel] without a preacher? And how will they preach unless they are sent? As it is written: 'How beautiful are the feet of those who preach the Good News of peace, who bring glad tidings of good things!" Paul is not describing a preacher by profession but any believer who proclaims the gospel. Notice, he portrays those who let their light shine in this way as having "beautiful feet!" We must use our feet to spread the good news with our words. We must go and speak to shine our lights.

The Roman saints had put a basket over every lamp in the church. Paul alludes to this when he wrote his letter to the Philippians describing how his boldness in shining the light even in chains had emboldened the Romans to shine theirs. In Philippians 1:14, he states, "And that most of the brothers in the Lord, being confident through my bonds, are more abundantly bold to speak the word of God without fear." He was in the midst of persecution and still shining his light. He was a prisoner awaiting a trial before the emperor.

While he was imprisoned, Paul was sharing the gospel of Jesus Christ with the servants of his household who came to care for him and the guards who were watching him. In the verse before, he writes, "Now I desire to have you know, brothers...the things which happened to me [persecution] have turned out rather to the progress of the Good News; so that it became evident to the whole palace guard, and to all the rest, that my bonds are in Christ." So, in that darkness, his light shined to those who cared for and guarded him. All could not have been interested in what he had to say at first, but Paul kept shining his light and they left the darkness.

What a blessing it would be to say after shining our lights all day, "The Lord made my feet beautiful today!" These are the beautiful feet of saints who shine their lights by sharing the gospel! We cannot dim our lights with baskets over our heads while men dwell in the darkness of error and sin. All need our lights. In Matthew 28:18-20, after Jesus resurrected from the dead, His final words encompassed the sharing of the gospel. Matthew records, "Jesus came to them and spoke to them, saying, 'All authority has been given to me in heaven and on earth. Go, and make disciples of all nations, baptizing them in the name of the Father and of the Son and of the Holy Spirit, teaching them to observe all things that I commanded you. Behold, I [Jesus] am with you always, even to the end of the age. Amen.'"

The Lord Jesus commanded His eleven disciples to make followers of Him. How? They were to go, baptize, and teach. This simply means that they were to go and then shine their lights. When people responded by receiving Christ as Savior and Lord, they were to baptize them. Then, they were to be taught the Holy Scriptures. We are to do the same.

Luke speaks of a second incident before Christ leaves the earth where once again, He tells His disciples to shine their lights. In Acts 1:8, the Lord declares, "But you will receive power when the Holy Spirit has come upon you. You will be witnesses to me in Jerusalem, in all Judea and Samaria, and to the uttermost parts of the earth." This also refers to all Christians. We are to shine our lights by sharing the good news. When the persecution of Saul broke out, this is exactly what they did. In Acts 8:3-4, Luke states, "But Saul ravaged the assembly, entering into every house, and dragged both men and women off to prison. Therefore, those who were scattered abroad went around preaching the word." Though they were persecuted, they shined their lights by "preaching the Word" everywhere they went.

So, we should shine our lights both verbally in the gospel and in our actions through our righteous lifestyles. Here are three suggestions to help us shine. If we follow these biblical principles, the Lord God will continually do His great work in whatever evangelistic efforts we may become involved in. This can lead to a full release of our bonds. Since we have discussed living a righteous life in a previous chapter, let us focus on shining the light of evangelism. How can we do this?

One way is to simply share the salvation message to those around us. In the New Testament, there are examples of many saints who simply went about proclaiming the good news in a simple, upfront way. In Acts 8:4, Luke writes that those who were scattered due to Saul's intense persecution went about and preached the gospel. The saints were scattered and shared the gospel. In Paul's letter of 1 Thessalonians 1:8, the apostle tells the church the Word of the Lord was declared in Macedonia and Achaia and wherever their faith toward God had gone out. The Thessalonian Christians were talking to people about the gospel wherever they were located.

There are other saints (including the apostles) who had a personal evangelistic strategy. They desired to establish a regular plan of action. This usually consisted of determining to whom they would witness and how they would make the opportunity to present the gospel. Matthew delineates the evangelistic strategy of John the Baptist in Matthew 3:1-6. John lived in the wilderness of Judea, dressed himself in camel's hair, ate locusts and honey, and proclaimed that the kingdom of God was at hand. This established him as one who was completely devoted to God and had made a special vow to demonstrate that commitment in a unique way. This contrasted John with the false overindulgent leaders of the day. Once, he had established this distinction, he was able to preach repentance. John adopted this strategy because he was a prophet (Matthew 11:9) and a forerunner of the message.

The Lord Jesus had His personal strategy of evangelism that He followed His entire ministry. In Matthew 4, the Lord Jesus traveled to the synagogue and to the marketplaces. He healed people and preached the kingdom. In Matthew 4:23, it says this, "Jesus went about in all Galilee, teaching in their synagogues, preaching the Good News of the Kingdom, and healing every disease and every sickness among the people. Paul's strategy was very similar.

In Acts 17:1-2 and verse 17, the historian Luke discloses that Paul's custom was to enter a city and begin preaching in the synagogue. Then he would go out into the marketplaces and proclaim the gospel. Why did Jesus (John 3:2) and Paul (Acts 22:3) have very similar evangelistic strategies? They were both recognized as rabbis. A visiting rabbi was allowed to speak in the synagogues. They went to the streets during the week to reach the Gentiles also. In the streets and market-places there was always much discussion of events, stories, religion, and politics. This was a place for open dialogue and sharing of ideas for all to hear. It was the perfect place for a preacher to present his message.

Peter's strategy is described in Acts 3:1-11. Peter simply healed and preached. He was not a rabbi and did not go into the synagogues. Why was Peter the one who preached to the crowds that gathered at Pentecost (Acts 2:14), after the healing of the lame man (Acts 3:12), and to the Sanhedrin (Acts 4:8) to name a few? There were other apostles with him, but he was the head of the group and a bold speaker. So, he stood up to preach the gospel.

Since Stephen and Philip were both Hellenistic Jews (Jews living in the Greek culture), they were able to minister to the many Greek speaking peoples. So, Stephen, the evangelist preached the good news to his people {the Jews) while Philip proclaimed the gospel to the Samaritans, an ethnic group that was similar to his, (half-Jew, half-Greek). Since they possessed supernatural abilities, they performed mighty miracles before they shared the gospel. They differed in that Stephen had a much more public ministry (refuting the Jews in public and also speaking before the Sanhedrin) and Philip a more private and personal ministry (sharing with Simon the Magician and then the Ethiopian Eunuch).

Apollos had a gifted intellect, was a powerful orator, and was mighty in the Scriptures. Since he was unafraid of large crowds, he frequently debated the Jews in public. He was able to refute their arguments for all to see (Acts 18:24-25). As one can see from these examples, they all had strategies, but they were very different. These approaches were based upon their language, backgrounds, gifts, and abilities.

We can also create our own personal evangelistic strategies to proclaim this good news. Perhaps those who are orphans may share the gospel and minister to orphans. Maybe those who have experienced a teen pregnancy might desire to bring the gospel to teens that are pregnant. The members of various professions could use their achievements as opportunities to give God glory and then share the gospel. An entrepreneur, musician, actor, artist, athlete, or physician might share their gratefulness for God's help and power when they achieve something. As they stand before an audience or are asked by others, the good news could be shared at that very moment. Some think mentioning the name of God is sufficient, but it is not. The Lord Jesus is the central focus of the good news.

Another way to share the gospel regularly is to view any and every situation as a possible evangelistic encounter. The Lord's apostles viewed almost every situation as a potential evangelistic encounter. Sometimes, they would create the opportunities to share the gospel. Other times, they took the opportunities when they came from the Spirit. In Acts 2, the day of Pentecost arrived, and the disciples were in the upper room praying. Suddenly, the Spirit came and there was the sound of a violent wind. Then, there came a manifestation of the tongues of fire resting above each one. This drew a big crowd. What did the apostles do? Peter and the others took this crucial opportunity that God had presented and shared the gospel. They took the opportunity when it came.

In Acts 3, Peter and John encountered a crippled man as they went into the temple to pray. When he asked for alms, they instead healed him. It isn't too difficult to assume that a lame man now walking would draw a large crowd. Once the crowd had gathered around this amazing event, the apostle preached the gospel. He made the opportunity to share the gospel. Previously, we saw that the miracles of Jesus drew crowds, and this created opportunities to preach the gospel. They were primarily to confirm His deity but also caused the crowds He needed to further His message.

In Acts 4, the apostle Peter was arrested and then brought before the Sanhedrin. Peter took the opportunity that was given to him and preached the gospel. In Acts 6-7, Stephen was arrested and dragged in before the Sanhedrin because he preached the gospel. This gave him another opportunity to preach it again to his accusers and he took it. In Acts 10, the Lord told Cornelius to send for Peter. Peter was given an opportunity from the Lord and took it. So, Peter traveled to Caesarea and proclaimed the gospel to Cornelius.

In Acts 16, Paul was arrested and imprisoned in Philippi. When an earthquake occurred, rather than escaping for his life, he utilized the situation to win the jailer and his whole household to Christ. This was not a specific opportunity that he planned. It was an opportunity he took. It is interesting that Paul allowed himself to be beaten and imprisoned. Since Paul was a Roman citizen, these actions were illegal. Perhaps,

Paul sensed God was at work and let the situation play itself out. In Acts 21:27, the Jews claimed the apostle Paul had allowed a Gentile to enter the holy temple and was arrested. Consequently, Paul took this sudden opportunity to share the good news with the crowd. From there, he preached the gospel of Christ to a series of prominent people: the High Priest, the Sanhedrin (Acts 23), Felix (Acts 24), Festus (Acts 25), and Herod Agrippa (Acts 26).

Before Festus in Acts 25:6-11, Paul invoked his right as a Roman citizen to appeal to Caesar and speak directly to the emperor. Every Roman citizen had this right, and Paul knew it. He obviously wanted to save this appeal for an opportune moment, if necessary. The apostle's subsequent journey to Rome had been previously prophesied to him on the road to Damascus by Jesus Himself (Acts 23:11).

After Festus asked the apostle Paul if he would be willing to go to Jerusalem to be judged, he knew the time had come. He was not only cognizant of this prophesy but had been informed that the Jews would attempt to ambush and kill him on the way. How else could the Lord have gotten His gospel to the courts of the most powerful man on earth? The apostle Paul had just made a critical opportunity to share the gospel. When he arrived in Rome, once again, he proclaimed the good news to anyone who would listen. Every situation became a potential encounter. He anticipated an opportunity in every negative situation. He knew that God could and did work anywhere Paul found himself.

How can believers make or take these many opportunities when they arrive? First, they should pray and then watch for open doors. Paul requested that the Colossians pray that God would open up a door for the Word in Colossians 4:3. Second, they must be alert and aware of circumstances that suddenly arise where the gospel can be proclaimed. These have been mentioned earlier in the examples of Peter. Third, the apostles expected God at any time to place them into situations in which they could make or take an opportunity. They were not caught off guard. The Lord Jesus told them that they would be His witnesses (Acts 1:8), and they expected God to work. Christians should expect and experience these same kind of things.

Fourth, evangelism was a way of life. Paul declared to the Corinthians that he did all things for the sake of the good news so he could become a fellow-partaker of the gospel (1 Corinthians 9:23). As the saints were persecuted in the city of Jerusalem, they fled. Everywhere these saints traveled, they preached the gospel (Acts 8: 4).

Another way that we can share the gospel is to tailor the good news to the moment. In the New Testament, the same essential saving elements are found in every presentation of the gospel. Yet, they were all very different. One will not find in the Scriptures any two gospel presentations which were exactly the same. In John 3:1-5, Nicodemus, an important teacher in Israel, came to the Lord Jesus to speak with Him. Jesus proclaimed the gospel using an analogy of spiritual birth. He must have a second spiritual birth with water and the Holy Spirit. Jesus expected Nicodemus to know the passage that He was referring to (Ezekiel 36:25-27). Here, God says He will cleanse His holy people with water and the Spirit to give them a new heart.

In John 4:6-10, Jesus was sitting at a well and proclaimed the gospel to a Samaritan woman who had come to draw some water. Christ described Himself as having living water (the gospel), which sprang into eternal life. The Samaritan woman was poor and ignorant of the Scriptures. He was sitting in front of a well. She had come to draw water. This became the perfect opportunity to utilize the situation to His advantage. He simply began to speak of a different kind of water that He could offer her.

Peter had a very different situation occur. In Acts 2:14-16, Luke records what had happened, "But Peter, standing up with the eleven, lifted up his voice, and spoke out to them, 'You men of Judea, and all you who dwell at Jerusalem, let this be known to you and listen to my words. For these aren't drunken, as you suppose, seeing it is only the third hour of the day. But this is what has been spoken through the prophet Joel.'" Peter began his presentation with what was happening at that very moment. There was a loud noise like a wind, and they were speaking in various languages they did not know. This was the fulfillment of a prophecy by the Holy Spirit. His listeners, who had gathered, were devout Jews who had come to celebrate Pentecost. They would have known the prophecy.

In Acts 3:12, Peter preached the gospel beginning with the power and name of Jesus who had been put to death and then rose from the dead. It was His power that healed the lame man who was now walking. There had been only a very short time since Christ's crucifixion. They would have been very familiar with the death of the Lord Jesus Christ. In Acts 8:26-35, evangelistic Philip met an Ethiopian eunuch on the road from Jerusalem. He was reading from Isaiah, and then Philip began his presentation in that particular passage. Since the eunuch was a God-fearing Gentile (Jew who adhered to the Jewish faith), he would have been familiar with prophecy.

In Acts 13:15-23, Paul entered a synagogue on the Sabbath in Pisidian Antioch and spoke from the prophecies in the Old Testament scrolls in front of him. He proclaimed God's powerful deliverance of Israel from Egypt, in the wilderness, in Canaan through the times of the judges, all throughout the entire era of the many kings, and now through the promised Messiah. In Nazareth, the Lord God also read from the Holy

Scriptures, but He proclaimed that He was the fulfillment of every single Old Testament prophecy (Luke 4:21). In both cases, their audiences would have been devout Jews who understood all these things.

In Acts 14:8-15, Paul arrived in Lystra and healed a lame man. A huge crowd gathered and declared them to be gods. Paul responded by preaching the gospel using creation as a starting point. Why? The apostle was speaking to heathens standing on the street who were polytheistic. It was better to start with creation. In Acts 17:23-34 Paul entered Athens and noticed a statue dedicated to an unknown god among many statutes of false deities. So, He proclaimed to the people that he had come to reveal the identity of this unknown god. Paul realized that these intellectuals did not want to offend any god, especially one that they may have forgotten and began his presentation there. In Acts 22:1-6, when the apostle Paul was arrested in Jerusalem for supposedly bringing a Gentile into the temple, Paul stood before a crowd of Jews and began with his personal testimony. He described how he came to Christ in their Hebrew language.

The good news is best proclaimed in response to a given situation and given context utilizing the essential elements of the gospel message. The presentation was weaved around the preacher, the one who was to hear it, and the situation in which they found themselves. Then, the gospel message was proclaimed. This does not mean that Christians do not have the right to begin heralding their message of salvation at any time in any place. This is what an ancient messenger would have done with a proclamation from a king. Why? This is how ancient leaders would communicate with their people.

The sharing of the gospel does not simply involve people being invited to church. This gospel must be preached. It is not the sole duty of the pastor but the duty of the flock. In Acts

1:8, Jesus left the disciples (and us) with these words, "But you will receive power when the Holy Spirit has come upon you. You will be witnesses to me in Jerusalem, in all Judea and Samaria, and to the uttermost parts of the earth."

When the persecution of Saul (Paul) erupted in full force, the saints were scattered. What did they do? As we saw, in Acts 8:4, Luke wrote this, "Therefore those [believers] who were scattered abroad went around preaching the word." When they ran for their lives, these believers preached the gospel wherever they went. The fruits of this sharing of the gospel will bring tremendous relief from our captivity as we see God use us to light their path to His kingdom.

As we now have seen, sharing the gospel with others aids in our spiritual growth. Being used by God to bring someone into the kingdom allows us to take our eyes off of ourselves and out on others. It stimulates us to read the Bible and pray more often. It encourages us to disciple young Christians and help them grow in their faith. As we support them, we will also grow because it will challenge us to be consistent in following the steps of growth ourselves. As we do this, we will find release from our captivity and bondage. This can produce calm, peace, joy, faith, comfort, hope, love, grace, courage, purpose, and trust.

Chapter 8

Utilize Your Spiritual Gifts

One of the most exciting aspects of the Christian life is the discovery and utilization of a believer's spiritual gifts. These are spiritual abilities that every believer possesses. The Spirit works through these gifts to do God's will. When Christians utilize their spiritual gifts, supernatural power is unleashed to build the saints up in the faith or to bring the unsaved to Christ according to God's will. When we become involved in ministering to the saints in the church or sharing the gospel in the world through the use of our spiritual gifts, we will experience some of the calm, peace, joy, faith, comfort, hope, love, grace, courage, purpose, and trust that we seek.

So, what are spiritual gifts? When we received Christ as Savior and Lord we were baptized into the Body of Christ. In 1 Corinthians 12:13, Paul explains, "For in one Spirit we were all baptized into one body, whether Jews or Greeks, whether bond or free; and were all given to drink into one Spirit." This baptism of the Spirit placed us into the kingdom of God as one people. At salvation, the Holy Spirit came to dwell within us. In 1 Corinthians 6:19, the apostle asks, "Or don't you know that your body is a temple of the Holy Spirit, which is in you, which you have from God? You are not your own." Therefore, the Spirit of our God resides in our spiritual bodies.

The Holy Spirit inside of us has given us spiritual gifts to be used by Him to work His power in the lives of others. These are spiritual abilities that may or may not relate to the skills we have developed in our lives. These are supernatural abilities for supernatural tasks. Our tasks help us build up the church and win the world to Christ (our purposes).

In 1 Corinthians 12:4-7, Paul provides for us a description of how these gifts operate. He writes, "Now there are various kinds of gifts, but the same Spirit. There are various kinds of service, and the same Lord. There are various kinds of workings, but the same God, who works all things in all. But to each one is given the manifestation of the Spirit for the profit of all." Paul asserts that there are a variety of spiritual gifts. They can be used for numerous kinds of ministries and have many different effects. Yet, they are all manifestations of the Holy Spirit. Though Christians are exercising different gifts in different ways with different outcomes, everyone is viewing the Holy Spirit at work.

This is all done for "the profit of all." This means they are given and utilized for the common good. They are not for our own use but should be only used for the good of others. These gifts are distributed to all the saints separately as the Holy Spirit desires. In 1 Corinthians 12:11, Paul writes, "But the one and the same [Holy] Spirit produces all of these, distributing to each one separately as he desires." When we are saved, we are given gifts based on the Spirit's will.

The gifts are given according to God's grace. In Romans 12:6, Paul describes this, "Having gifts differing according to the grace that was given to us, if prophecy, let us prophesy according to the proportion of our faith." Also, they provide God's grace to others as we use them. In 1 Peter 4:10, we are told, "As each has received a gift, employ it in serving one another, as good managers of the grace of God in its various forms." Gifts are the dispensing of the grace of God to others through us. So, it is important that we learn what gifts God has given us and how to use them. Christians must focus on ministries that can utilize their giftedness as God leads.

The Spirit has placed many different people with different gifts, effects, and results in different kinds of churches. Paul compares the church to the body and explains that just as a body has different parts (such as the eyes, feet, and hands), so the church, the Body of Christ, also needs different gifts to function. In 1 Corinthians 12:14-20, he writes, "For the body is not one member, but many. If the foot would say, 'Because I'm not the hand, I'm not part of the body,' it is not therefore not part of the body. If the ear would say, 'Because I'm not the eye, I'm not part of the body,' it's not therefore not part of the body. If the whole body were an eye, where would the hearing be? If the whole were hearing, where would the smelling be? But now God has set the members, each one of them, in the body just as he desired. If they were all one member, where would the body be? But now they are many members, but one body." Every gifted member is important to the proper function of the local body of Christ.

This means that we must be a part of a local congregation to minister our gifts. If we are not, then we are making the church function as if it were missing a body part with the other parts having to compensate for the loss. Also, we can't exalt Christians who possess the more showy gifts and more expansive ministries with greater results. Nor can we shun the saints who may have the "behind the scenes" gifts with smaller ministries and results. All are critical to the proper functioning of the body of Christ. In fact, in verses 21-26, Paul argues that the parts of the body deemed much "less honorable" may be far more important, "The eye can't tell the hand, 'I have no need for you,' or again the head to the feet, 'I have no need for you.' No, much rather, those members of the body which seem to be weaker are necessary. Those parts of the body which we think to be less honorable, on those we [Christians] bestow more abundant honor; and our unpresentable parts have more abundant propriety; whereas our presentable parts have no such need."

At the end of verses 24-26, the apostle concludes, "But God composed the body together, giving more abundant honor to the inferior part, that there should be no division in the body, but that the members should have the same care for one another. When one member suffers, all the members suffer with it....one member is honored, all...members rejoice with it." We accept the gifts we are given and honor the gifts others are given. We do not compare ourselves to others as if one had better gifts, because they are all important.

Miraculous and prophetic gifts were used to prove and verify the truth of the good news, write some of the gospels and the letters of the New Testament, rebuke the Jews for their hardness of heart, and also provide instruction on the apostle's teaching. These were temporary and have now ceased. They quietly died out as those who possessed them passed from this life. We know this because the true gifts would be manifested in exactly the same manner today as they were in the age of the apostles. Yet, they are not.

The temporary gifts are found in several passages in the Bible. In 1 Corinthians 12:8-10, Paul describes some of these, "For to one is given through the Spirit the word of wisdom, and to another the word of knowledge, according to the same Spirit; to another faith, by the same Spirit; and to another gifts of healings, by the same Spirit; and to another workings of miracles; and to another prophecy; and to another discerning of spirits; to another different kinds of languages; and to another the interpretation of languages." The gift of faith, healing, and working of miracles were, as the names indicate, miraculous gifts. The gifts of knowledge, prophecy, wisdom, [known] languages, the interpretation of [known] languages, and discerning of [demon] spirits were prophetic. This means that God spoke directly through them while they were using their gifts. All these gifts have ceased because those who possessed them have passed away.

A description of the gifts, which are present today for all of us, can be found in 1 Corinthians 12:27-30. Here among the temporary gifts, The apostle Paul lists the permanent ones: teaching, helps, and administration. In Romans 12:6-8, Paul lists service, encouragement, giving, leading, and mercy. Some may have more than one of these gifts, but all Christians will have one. The church or evangelistic team should create and build its many ministries around the gifts of the saints in a congregation. If there are believers with the gift of mercy, then the church should develop several mercy ministries to both the unsaved in order to share the gospel and the saved to build them up in the faith. These ministries should be led by one with the gift of leadership and another administration. So, it is important to figure out where each of us fits in.

Here is one example. If several saints desire to share the gospel and build up the saints in a senior residence, they will need different gifts. Those Christians with the gifts of mercy and encouragement should sit among the residents and speak individually with each of them. Christians with the gift of helps might attend and be prepared for emergencies. Those Christians who serve would handle the setting up of chairs, music equipment, etc. Those with the gift of teaching would provide the instruction. Saints with the gift of giving would finance the ministry. The one in charge would be a leader and the one who managed it would be an administrator. All of these people would focus on sharing the gospel to the unsaved and building up the Christian faith of the saved.

There is no specific method we are given in the Scriptures to discover our spiritual gifts. Since they are "manifestations of the Spirit," then they should be present when we are filled with the Spirit. In Ephesians 5:18, Paul commands, "Don't be drunken with wine...which is dissipation, but be filled with the Spirit." In verses 19-21, the apostle Paul adds what the results will be, "speaking to one another in psalms, hymns, and spiritual songs; singing...making melody in your heart to the Lord; giving thanks always concerning all things in the name of our Lord Jesus Christ, to God, even the Father; subjecting yourselves to one another in the fear of Christ." So, being controlled by the Spirit brings a song to our hearts, a word of gratitude to our lips, and the mutual subjecting of ourselves to one another. This refers to mutual ministry and service to one another. As we do this, our spiritual abilities will become active whether we realize it or not.

The best way to discern the spiritual gift we may have is to search our desires. We may ask, "What do I desire to do for the Lord?" Then, we would proceed through the gifts and decide which of these fits best with our desires. If we have the gift of teaching, we will want to study, interpret, instruct, and apply the Word in people's lives. If we possess the gift of service, we will want to faithfully and diligently support the ministries of the church and meet the needs of others by doing a variety of tasks that are spiritually based. If we have the gift of encouragement, we will desire to come alongside others to biblically comfort, guide, and gently push them in a holy direction. Those Christians who have the leadership gift will want to provide a biblical vision and leadership.

We should examine our desires in the light of the other gifts also. Those who have the gift of administration want to organize and manage others in the ministry. The ones with the gift of giving desire to support ministries financially or meet the personal needs of others. The Lord provides them with the money necessary and the gift to give it away. If we have the gift of mercy, we will constantly be on the alert for hurting desperate people. Then, we will come alongside them and help. The gift of helps is similar to service but people with this gift will thrive in a time of great crises or emergency, and this is important for the saints.

All of these gifts can be expressed in a variety of ways to many different individuals and groups who are of numerous ages. Most importantly, they all must involve the principles of God's Word and prayer. This means that as we minister whatever gifts we have been given, the Word of God must be shared if possible and we should prayerfully serve the saints.

Another way to determine our spiritual gift (s) is to look for the fruit produced when we do ministry that would utilize the gift. In 1 Corinthians 12:6-7, the apostle Paul describes the "various kinds of workings [effects]...who works all things in all. But to each one is given the manifestation of the Spirit for the profit of all." Here, the apostle Paul explains that our gifts will produce different kinds of effects for the profit of all. So, a second way to determine our gifts is to look at the effects and spiritual profit of the gift we think we may have on the people to whom we minister. We should observe the Holy Spirit at work through the growth in Christ that is produced.

In Romans 1:13, Paul writes, "Now I don't desire to have you unaware, brothers, that I often planned to come to you, and was hindered so far, that I might have some fruit among you also, even as among the rest of the Gentiles." Paul was ministering using his gifts and expected to see the fruit of it among the Roman Christians as he had seen among those of other churches. As we minister, we should seek feedback.

Another way, to ascertain our gifts is to ask others. As we use our gifts in service, we should seek confirmation from those to whom we minister, the similarly gifted, the wise, and the elders of the church. The Holy Spirit will guide us also by these saints in our lives. This is so important, because we can deceive ourselves into the thinking that we have a gift we simply do not have, and this can lead to many problems. The following are suggestions to confirm gifts.

First, we should seek confirmation by these who practice the same gifts that we may have. In the church at Corinth, the saints were horribly mismanaging the weekday gatherings. There were too many similarly gifted saints speaking, too many interrupting, and too many with the wrong message. The church service was confusing and disorderly. One of the safeguards Paul puts into place was the confirmation of the message and ministry by the similarly gifted. In his letter to the Corinthians, he writes, "Let the prophets speak, two or three, and let the others discern" (1 Corinthians 14:29). Here, Paul allows only two or three prophets to speak. Then, the other prophets would confirm their message or keep them in check if they misused the gifts. We need the same to occur to confirm us. For example, if we have the gift of mercy, those with a similar gift should confirm that we have the gift.

Second, we should seek the opinion of those in the church who are wise. In Proverbs 1:5, Solomon writes, "That the wise man may hear, and increase in learning; that the man of understanding may attain to sound counsel." In Proverbs 15:22, the king adds, "Where there is no counsel, plans fail; but in a multitude of counselors they are established." He explains that wise people will certainly seek sound counsel from other wise people. They will desire to hear, learn, and understand. This includes our giftedness. To be wise, we should find those who are wise and ask them to observe our ministries and confirm our gifts.

Third, we should request confirmation by church elders. These leaders have spiritual responsibility for us. They are the overseers of the church. In Acts 20:28, Paul warned the elders in Ephesus, "Take heed, therefore, to yourselves, and to all the flock, in which the Holy Spirit has made you overseers, to shepherd the assembly of the Lord...God which he purchased with his own blood." In Hebrews 13:17, the author of the book described the responsibility of church elders and our response to them, "Obey your leaders and submit to them, for they watch on behalf of your souls, as those who will give account, that they may do this with joy, and not with groaning [from lack of obedience], for that would be unprofitable for you." The utilization of our spiritual gifts would be included in the "watching over our souls." The asking for gift confirmation would definitely be included in "obeying and submitting" to them.

Fourth, we should seek the opinions of Christian family members. This means if we are married, we should seek the confirmation of our spouses. Genesis 2:24 states, "Therefore a man will leave his father and his mother, and will join with his wife, and they will be one flesh." Since husbands and wives become a partnership, they should seek confirmation by the other partner.

If we are young enough to be living at home with our parents, then we are truly under their authority. This would include the confirmation of our spiritual gifts. In Ephesians 6:1, Paul declares, "Children, obey your parents in the Lord, for this is right." Then in verse 4, he adds, "You fathers, don't provoke your children to wrath [make them angry], but nurture them in the discipline [training] and instruction of the Lord." The gifts should be taught through their instruction and used with their guidance. In Proverbs 1:8, Solomon says, "My son, listen to your father's instruction, and don't forsake your mother's teaching." Then, in Proverbs 6:20, he reiterates, "My son, keep your father's commandment, and don't forsake your mother's teaching."

If we follow these steps, we will mightily be used of God. As in evangelism, ministering to others with our gifts aids in our spiritual growth. Being used by God to perhaps help others find freedom from their captivity will allow us to take our eyes off ourselves and put them on others. As we use our gifts to support others, we will grow because it will challenge us to be consistent in following the steps of growth. ourselves.

Chapter 9

Expect a Spiritual Battle

As we grow into the stature of Jesus, we will increasingly be able to overcome many of the obstacles that life can bring our way. Though these may initially bind us in the shackles of a broken heart, emptiness, pain, desperation, regret, guilt, despair, anxiety, a lack of purpose, or financial uncertainty, we can find victory over them. Yet, we must understand that numerous battles may have to be fought with the final great victory being death itself when we are released from our physical body, the influence of the world system, and the temptation of the Devil.

These three are the reasons there is a battle to be fought as we attempt to overcome the issues we face. Though we are true believers and saved by faith, we must still reside in unredeemed bodies, live in sinful societies, and encounter an adversary named Satan. As a result, we must battle all three of these enemies to overcome our difficulties. Accomplishing this momentous task requires much time, fierce battles, and supernatural strength. Since victories on a real battlefield are hard fought, then we must also be ready to fight hard on the battlefield of our hearts and minds.

To overcome these three formidable foes, we must put on the full armor of God. This armor is discussed at length by Paul in Ephesians 6:10-20. Paul describes our need to be strong through God's armor. In Ephesians 6:10-11, he asserts, "Finally, be strong in the Lord and in the strength of His might. Put on the full armor of God, so that you will be able to stand firm against the schemes of the devil." The Greek word translated "put on" means "to sink into or to put on as clothing." By faith, Christians are to spiritually put on each and every piece of armor one at a time, just as warriors would physically put on their armor for battle. Then, they will fight with the supernatural strength of the Lord. Why? Our armor is spiritual and divinely powerful (2 Corinthians 10:4).

The armor will enable us to "stand firm." The Greek word translated "stand firm" means "to stay in its place, to stop and stand still." It pictures soldiers in battle not giving up even one foot of ground to their enemies. Warriors will hold their ground and not allow advancement. Spiritually, this means the enemy will not make any advances to add to or keep us in bondage. How does this actually work? The battle is raging, and the enemy begins to make his advances. We will start to succumb to fear, anxiety, despair, desperation, regret, guilt, loneliness, or uncertainty. So, immediately, we put on the full armor of God, then fight the battle against those debilitating feelings, and find victory. Finally, relief will come.

Though Paul defines here the enemy as the Devil, we also know that the Devil has created a world of minions involved in his world system (society) that follow him. Also, within us is an enemy which is the flesh. The Devil and his demons develop many "schemes" to shackle us further and throw us into a downward spiral of defeat. The Greek word translated "schemes" refers to deceitful methods, cunning trickery, and crafty ways to crush us. So, we must be aware of everything happening around us that unbeknownst to us may trigger a bad feeling, habit, or addiction which might send us into a free fall.

In Ephesians 6:12, Paul describes these forces of evil that wage war against us, "For our struggle is not against flesh and blood, but against the rulers, against the powers, against the world forces of this darkness, against the spiritual forces of wickedness in the heavenly places." We must continually remind ourselves that this battle is not against humans even if they are instigating or inciting the problems. It is the dark power behind them. This is an organized army of demons with various ranks, positions, and responsibilities. They are like no enemy on earth but far worse. Their goal is to damn souls to hell for all eternity as they themselves are damned (Matthew 25:41).

How can they accomplish this? Their main method is to render us powerless, so we will not evangelize the lost and build them up in the faith when they do become Christians. In our context, they may fill us with emptiness, fear, despair, desperation, or uncertainty. They may cause others to break our hearts, destroy us financially, take away our careers, and disrupt our ministries which adds to our burdens, keeps us preoccupied, and ruins our witness.

In Ephesians 6:13, Paul portrays this battle again from a different angle, "Therefore, take up the full armor of God, so that you will be able to resist in the evil day, and having done everything, to stand firm." The key to winning this evil battle is "resisting." The Greek word translated "resist" refers to "setting oneself against, withstanding, or opposing." We must set ourselves against the temptation to succumb to our bondage, not fight back, or give up.

In Ephesians 6:14-20, Paul repeats his declaration to stand firm and then describes the armor we are to put on in order to resist these temptations that the Devil throws at us. Each piece of armor is critical to the battle we must face. Let us look at the defensive armor first from top to bottom. Paul mentions the "helmet of salvation." The soldier had to put his helmet on to protect his head. A blow to the head by a sword would kill him instantly. This refers to the salvation of the person and acknowledging he or she must act as if they are saved. In Romans 13:12, Paul explains, "The night is far gone, and the day is near. Let's therefore throw off the deeds of darkness, and let's put on the armor of light." In this biblical context, we determine we are saved and will act like those who have received Christ rather than those who have not in dealing with our captivity.

Second, the breastplate of righteousness should be taken up. This is generally the confession of sin and the pursuit after righteous deeds. In 2 Timothy 2:22, Paul tells Timothy, "Flee from youthful lusts; but pursue righteousness, faith, love, and peace with those who call on the Lord out of a pure heart." In our context, we must pursue after solutions to our problems that will not plunge us into various kinds of sins: drugs, alcohol, sexual promiscuity, adultery, and other evil deeds to medicate the problem. Instead, we will commit to practicing the principles of the Christian life despite our many feelings or circumstances. Then, we should determine that we will grow spiritually, walk intentionally, study consistently, pray persistently, live righteously, fellowship steadily, utilize our gifts, evangelize regularly, and confess humbly. After this, we should see a loosening of the chains that bind us. We should experience a resultant freedom.

Third, soldier saints are to "gird their loins with truth" in their battle. The Roman soldier had to roll his long garb up and tighten it with a belt in order to fight. This does not refer to honesty but the knowledge and understanding of God's truth in the Scriptures. This is so critical in the battles we must face. The Christian warrior must really know the truth of God and not be fooled by Satan's many lies which are hurled fast and furious at the believer (John 8:44). In 1 John 2:14, the apostle describes those who are spiritually mature, "I have written to you, fathers, because you know him who is from the beginning. I have written to you, young men, because you are strong, and the word of God remains in you, and you have overcome the evil one."

These mature Christians knew the Word of God and were able to "overcome the Evil One." The Greek Word translated "overcome" means to conquer or prevail against someone or something. We must know the Word because the flesh, the world, and the Devil will lie to us. They will encourage us to become angry, bitter, "stand up for our rights," and then "pay them back for what they did." In our context, we must know the principles which govern any situation well enough to discern at every point what the Scriptures say about the issues we are facing and what to do about them.

Fourth, God's warrior must have the appropriate shoes. His feet must be "shod with the gospel of peace." The Roman soldier wore a cleat-like shoe into battle, so he could never lose his footing. These special shoes had spikes under them to entrench the feet into the ground for balance in the time of battle. These are similar to the cleats a football player wears on the football field. They utilize them for much needed traction and balance. This refers to the full understanding of the gospel and the regular and consistent sharing of it. When we are interested in winning people to Christ, we will be able to take our focus off our own problems and turn it upon others. Also, we will not be quick to medicate ourselves in sinful practices to alleviate the pain because we need to be an example to those to whom we are sharing.

Fifth, these spiritual warriors are to defend themselves with "the shield of faith." These shields were big enough to hide behind and take the blows of a sword and the slings of arrows. A shield was covered with pitch and immediately could extinguish the flaming arrows of an enemy archer. In Ephesians 6:16, Paul actually describes the temptations of the Devil as "flaming arrows of the evil one." The picture is of archers who have shot arrows into a crowd of warriors to maim or kill them. Their hope was for them to become confused, terrorized, and retreat from the battle. At times, the arrows will come so quickly toward us that we will not be able catch our breath. The Devil, Satan, will want us to stumble and stagger spiritually and fall into sin as we handle our difficulties. We will stand firm behind the shield of faith to extinguish them.

We must do battle with a grounded, steadfast faith. As we face our issues, we will live by faith, not feeling. We cannot let our experiences control us. We will believe the promises of God's Word and follow its principles. We will subject our feelings to our faith. Then, we face our issues knowing that God is in control and protects us no matter what we face.

There are also two offensive weapons for our numerous spiritual battles. The first is "the sword of the spirit, which is the Word of God." The Greek word translated "Word" means specific utterances of the Word. In 1 Peter 1:25, Peter uses the identical word when he writes, "'But the Word of the Lord endures forever.' And this is the word which was preached to you." This refers to the specific words of the Scriptures that apply to a particular situation. A warrior in battle is always attacking with his sword. In Matthew 4, each temptation of the Devil was met with a specific verse from the Scriptures.

We battle the rationalizations of the flesh with the truth of Scriptures. We should have a conversation within ourselves between the old man (the flesh in our bodies) and the new man (our true selves in Christ). We compare our thoughts, words, and actions with biblical principles. The flesh will counter with all kinds of reasons why we should follow our own urges, the world's wisdom, or the Devil's temptations to solve our problems. We must decide who we will follow: God or our flesh. We should ask the question, "Will I become obedient to my new master or old master? When we pursue after Christ in our Christian lives and practice His principles, we will gain insight into His Word and be able to challenge

106

the flesh with biblical principles. This will be far easier if we know the Scriptures well, will it not?

To battle a fear of death, physical pain, emptiness, regret, tragedy, guilt, despair, broken hearts, anxiety, aimlessness, and financial uncertainty, we should find Scripture passages that concern themselves with these issues and follow them. If our flesh desires to find solutions in its lusts, the world, or the Devil, we find Bible verses that command against them. Then, we battle. As we are engaged in this furious exchange, we should pick up what I call "the spear of prayer." Though Paul does not borrow this image, I like to use it as an aid in my remembrance of the second offensive weapon - prayer.

Paul finishes his discussion of the battle with prayer. In Ephesians 6:18-20, he implored, "With all prayer and petition pray at all times in the Spirit, and with this in view, be on the alert with all perseverance and petition for all the saints, and pray on my behalf, that utterance may be given to me in the opening of my mouth, to make known with boldness the mystery of the gospel." In the midst of the battle the warrior is communicating constantly with the commander and with the other warriors in battle. Each is supporting the other as they follow the commands of their leader. When they need help, they ask for it; when others need help, they ask for it.

In 1 Thessalonians 5:25, in the midst of the raging battle with the forces of evil, Paul cried out, "Brothers, pray for us." In Romans 1:9, he continues with these words, "For God is my witness, whom I serve in my spirit in the Good News of his Son, how unceasingly I make mention of you always in my prayers." As the apostle Paul was battling and they were battling, both of them were praying for each other. In our context, as warriors, we pray for victory against the flesh, the world, the Devil, and God's assistance in the coping process. We can also pray that the Spirit will empower us to practice the principles of the Christian life in order to grow in Christ. This strong and powerful offensive weapon cannot be left out of our combat. It is essential for victory.

To find victory in battle, we must know our enemies. The first enemy is within us. To release us from our chains, we must understand "the flesh." In Romans 7:20, Paul calls our flesh the "sin which dwells in me." Residing in us is a powerful and influential "sin principle" that we carry with us twenty-four hours a day. This sin principle causes our physical bodies to desire and lust after every kind of evil we can imagine. The flesh (common word for this principle) desires to wallow in its own sin. It can be prideful, arrogant, and boastful, but it could also be insecure, worried, and desperate. It could bring much pain, guilt, regret, sorrow, misery, and many other feelings that can cause or add to our bondage. It can chastise us like a vicious parent. It will whip saints with the memories of their own mistakes. It could bring deep feelings of inadequacy and hopelessness as we attempt to face challenges before us.

In the movies, when someone struggles with doubts, on one shoulder is a little demon and on the other shoulder a small angel. Each of them is vying for attention and giving advice. This is not the case in real life. Instead, in our own minds, it is the "old man" accusing us, while the "new man" excuses us through the Holy Spirit. In Ephesians 4:22-24, the apostle discusses this old and new life (man). Paul writes concerning the old life we lived, "That you put away, as concerning your former way of life, the old man, that grows corrupt after the lusts of deceit." Then he contrasts this with the new man, "And that you be renewed in the spirit of your mind, and put on the new man, who in the likeness of God has been created in righteousness and holiness of truth." When we became Christians, we put on this "new man" (or woman). We became brand new creations in Jesus Christ (1

Corinthians 5:17). So, the feelings and responses that may dominate our minds and torment us do not come from the Spirit in the new man. The voices inside us which attempt to berate, cry out in regret and guilt, speak fearful, despairing, or even desperate words are the moans and groans of the flesh. It is the "old man" in us.

Paul writes that we must do battle with this flesh of ours. In 1 Corinthians 9, he uses a boxing analogy to explain how he himself handled this ugly sin principle inside himself. In verse 27, he describes, "But I beat my body and bring it into submission, lest by any means, after I have preached to others, I myself should be rejected." The word "beat" in the Greek means "to beat black and blue." In our case, it would refer to hard effort to fight back against the lies of the flesh. We must fight against the "old man."

The second enemy is the "world." This refers to the society of people who are not saved. In 1 John 2:15-17, John writes, "Don't love the world or the things that are in the world. If anyone loves the world, the Father's love isn't in him. For all that is in the world, the lust of the flesh, the lust of the eyes, and the pride of life, isn't the Father's, but is the world's. The world is passing away with its lusts, but he who does God's will remain forever." Societies are focused on what the eyes desire, what the body craves, and what everyone wants to boast about. Their end is always the accumulation of wealth, power, influence, and the satisfaction of all their appetites. Though it appears as if they truly desire to release us from our problems, issues, and maladies; instead, it profits them to allow us to remain in our chains. We must take some time to seriously consider this real possibility.

Why would they do this? They sell more drugs (over the counter, prescription, and illegal). They involve us in solving our problems through every kind of evil that they can profit from in music, videos, and social media. Those tormented will more likely buy their books, attend their conferences, and stay at their expensive retreats. More anguish leads to more physical problems, which fill their hospitals, surgery rooms, and specialty care centers. We must do battle with our society to reject their human wisdom and predatory behavior. Then, we can find solutions in God first and filter through their man-made methods to aid us in our battle. We do know that physicians, counselors, and others can provide help in dealing with our issues. Yet, we must keep a wary eye out for treatments and solutions based on theory rather than fact, a wisdom that is contrary to God's, and nefarious motives by those in authority above them. This is where our battle with the world lies.

The world is desperate for the proclamation of the plan of redemption. Consider the condition of those who come into a Christian's life and do not know Christ. First, they are born in rebellion to God. David declared in Psalm 51:5 that he was brought forth in iniquity and conceived in sin. Man is born with the sin principle which has an innate propensity for evil. In Romans 7:14, The apostle Paul felt such a conflict within himself that he described it as being of the flesh and sold into bondage to sin.

Second, unbelievers live lives devoted and committed to sin. The unsaved live by sinful values and attitudes resulting in sinful actions. In Romans 6:17, Paul describes this sinful lifestyle, when he declares that the Roman Christians were slaves to sin in their former lives before Christ. In Ephesians 2:2, Paul describes the constant sin of the unsaved by stating that they walk according to the course of this world, which is according to the Devil, the prince of the power of the air, and are sons of disobedience. When people do not know the Lord Jesus, they are following the Devil and his ways. Satan is their ruler, and they are his slaves.

Third, Satan's kingdom is called the domain of darkness in Colossians 1:13. Every unbeliever lives in this domain and stumbles in this darkness. 1 John 1:6 states, "If we say that we have fellowship with him and walk in the darkness, we lie, and don't tell the truth." The apostle John calls this walking in darkness. Therefore, they are completely spiritually dead. In Ephesians 2:1, Paul reveals to the Ephesians that they had been dead in their trespasses and sin before coming to the Savior. Later in the letter, chapter 4:17-18, he explains this condition as being futile in their own minds, darkened in understandings, and alienated from God's life.

The Scriptures describe with many details this terrifying condition that unbelief produces. These poor people have no forgiveness of sins (Colossians 1:14). They are unrighteous (Romans 3:10), children of God's wrath (Ephesians 2:3), and captive by their own desires (Galatians 5:19-21). They have problems but no real solutions to their difficulties (James 1:2-4). They have human friendships but no bond that is eternal and spiritual (1 Corinthians 12:25).

When true believers come to Christ through the power of the Holy Spirit, their whole lives change. The Lord transforms them from rebellion to praise (Ephesians 1:12), turns them from a life totally devoted to sin to a life devoted to holiness (Romans 7:24-25), and turns them from their captivity to sin to freedom in the Holy Spirit (Romans 8:9-10). They are made spiritually alive (Ephesians 2:5) and given the forgiveness of sins (Acts 10:43). These children of wrath become children of God (John 1:12), are declared righteous before Him (Romans 5:19), and will now experience love, joy, peace and the rest of the fruits of the Spirit (Galatians 5:22-23).

The person who does not know the Lord must live a life centered on sinful values, motivated by sinful attitudes, and committed to sinning as a pattern of their lives. Christians know that He is the solution to every problem, the answer to every dilemma, and the way of coping with every difficulty (Philippians 1:20). As a result, in all their relationships with unbelievers, the sharing of the good news must come first. Trouble will never leave a life filled with sin that is destined for judgment. These dear people are desperate for Christ to meet their innermost longings and outer most needs.

The third enemy is the Devil, and he has schemes. He is the Serpent of Old who loves to find God's people and test their loyalty (Job 1:11), tempt them to sin (Luke 22:31), or incite their flesh to behave like the "old man" (Galatians 2:11-14). This way they will remain captive and never find freedom in Christ. He will do everything in his power with a myriad of fallen angels to influence us to become depressed, defeated, grief-stricken, angry, bitter, or immobilized.

In 1 Thessalonians 2:17-18, he described how he wanted to come to them more than once, but Satan thwarted him. He describes this, "But we, brothers, being bereaved of you for a short season, in presence, not in heart, tried even harder to see your face with great desire, because we wanted to come to you - indeed, I, Paul, once and again - but Satan hindered us." Paul knew the schemes and flaming missiles of the Devil aimed toward those who know Jesus Christ. He also knew the evil intentions and battle plans directed at those who were about to enter the kingdom of God. If the saints become fully committed to witnessing or ministry, Satan will take notice.

Satan is a powerful evil angelic being. In Scripture, Satan is called the Great Dragon and the Serpent of Old (Revelation 12:9), the Prince of the Power of the Air (Ephesians 2:2), the Evil One (1 John 3:12), the Father of Lies (John 8:44) as well as other designations. As true believers present the good news and minister to the saints, they may battle this formidable, supernatural adversary. Satan has developed some specific strategies and schemes in his attempt to build a kingdom of his own and to become higher than the Most High (Isaiah 14, Ezekiel 28).

His approach is found in 1 Peter 5:8, where Peter declares that Satan is the adversary, who behaves like a roaring lion seeking someone to devour. Would not the perfect target be all Christians who are sharing the gospel and pulling people out of his dark kingdom or helping people grow in Christ? We cannot afford to be ignorant of the Devil's schemes or we will allow him to outwit us. We should not overestimate his power or underestimate God's sovereign control (Job 1-2). In 1 John 4:4, John writes, "You are of God, little children, and have overcome them; because greater is he who is in you than he who is in the world." The Holy Spirit in us is greater than the Serpent who is in the world. No matter what the Devil and his demons throw at us, we can handle it through the power of the Holy Spirit. There are numerous schemes Satan has developed in his wicked opposition to believers.

First, the Serpent seeks to influence us in the same way he did with the disciples of the Lord. In Matthew 16:22-23, Jesus declared that He would suffer, be killed, and then be raised up on the third day. Peter strongly disagreed. He declared that this would never happen to the Lord. Christ's reply was to rebuke the Devil, who had been behind Peter's foolish remark. In Luke 22:31-32, Christ told Peter and the other disciples that Satan had asked the Father permission to sift them like wheat and it had been granted to him by God. The disciples would be scattered, but the Devil had something special planned for Peter. Before the next sunrise, he would be challenged and deny Christ three times.

Lucifer has attention focused on the Lord's disciples and destroying them as the Lord was arrested. In Luke 22:31-32, the historian records, "The Lord said, 'Simon, Simon, behold,

Satan asked to have you, that he might sift you as wheat, but I prayed for you, that your faith wouldn't fail. You, when once you have turned again, establish your brothers.'" Then, Jesus comforted Peter with the knowledge that He had prayed for him. After he turned back to the Lord, Peter was to strengthen his brothers. This was fulfilled in the denial of the Lord three times (Luke 22:34; Matthew 26:69-75).

Second, Satan propagates lies. In 2 Corinthians 11:14-15, Paul asserts that Satan disguises himself to look like an angel of light. The word light refers to truth and holiness revealed. It has a moral and a doctrinal aspect to it. Its opposite is evil and error (darkness). He dresses himself up to look exactly like messengers of the truth and dresses his servants up like ministers of righteousness. His strategy is simple. While the true light is shining, he will put up false lights all around the true one. These false lights in the guise of attractive messiahs and prophets who will teach doctrines that cater to men's lusts. This is why there are so many false religions.

As we have seen, numerous battles may have to be fought as we seek to grow into the stature of Jesus Christ. As we persist in battle and find victory after victory, we can slowly and meticulously loosen the shackles of the broken hearts, emptiness, pain, desperation, regret, guilt, despair, anxiety, lack of purpose, or financial uncertainty that binds us. In its place will come calm, peace, joy, faith, comfort, hope, love, grace, courage, purpose, and trust. The final victory of death will provide an eternity of freedom.

Chapter 10

Confess with A Humble Attitude

As we attempt to walk as Christians in order to release our captive hearts from our fear, pain, emptiness, regret, tragedy, guilt, despair, broken hearts, anxiety, aimlessness, and uncertainty, we will stumble and fall along the way. The old habits of coping are hard to give up. The temptations of developing new approaches to deal with the issues we face that are sinful are great. No matter how much we desire not to sin, we will. As a result, we must be prepared to stumble, fall, confess, and begin the walk again. This may occur many times a day at first, but as we grow in Christ it decreases.

It is important to note that repentance does not end at the moment of salvation. True believers in Christ will constantly be recognizing the sins that they are committing and asking God for forgiveness. This is not just an eternal issue but a relational one. When we received Christ as Savior and Lord, all of our sins were forgiven from the past, present, and future (Colossians 2:13-14; Romans 8:1). In our relationship with the Lord Jesus upon this earth in the flesh, we still confess our transgression. This restores our relationship with the Lord God in a relational sense. Then, any barriers between us and God are eliminated.

John speaks to this in his first letter. Some were saying in the church that they had matured to such a level that they no longer sinned in any way. John, the apostle, counters with a scathing response. In 1 John 1:8, the apostle emphatically states, "If we say that we have no sin, we deceive ourselves, and the truth is not in us." Then in verse 10, he declares, "If we say that we haven't sinned, we make him a liar, and his word is not in us." Those who claimed that they had never sinned or no longer sinned were simply lying to themselves, others, and God. The truth of His Righteous Word was not in them because His truth convicts us of sin.

Then sandwiched between these two convicting passages is what believers do when they realize they have sinned. In verse 9, he proclaims, "If we confess our sins, He is faithful and righteous to forgive us the sins, and to cleanse us from all unrighteousness." The verbs "confess" and "forgive" are in the present tense which indicates continual action in present time. Believers are continually confessing their sins and the Lord God is continually forgiving them. Repentance and asking God to forgive us is a lifelong practice. This is so important.

Our sins might be a part of the underlying cause of the captivity we feel. Or, it may be adding our bondage as we depend on our lusts to provide relief and release rather than God. As we repent of our many sins and experience God's constant forgiveness, we continue our righteous walk in Him. This will not only greatly help in our problems but also glorify our Savior and Lord.

There are three aspects to the full concept of "repentance" in the Scripture. These are presented in various places by different writers in the New Testament. Repentance involves admitting the many sins we have committed, sorrowing and mourning over their wickedness, and turning away from them toward righteousness. All of these are crucial elements in the repentance process and should be anticipated as the Spirit convicts us of our sin.

The first is the admission of sin. To fully repent, we must admit that we have sinned. This means that Christians are to acknowledge that their wicked thoughts, words, and actions were indeed sins. Notice 1 John 1:9 again, "If we confess our sins, He is faithful and righteous to forgive us the sins, and to cleanse us from all unrighteousness." John uses a critical word to explain his meaning. The Greek word translated "confess" literally means "to say the same thing." Confession is to say the same thing about a thought, word, or action that God says about them; that is, they are sinful and against God's law.

When Jesus encountered a rich young ruler, he claimed to have kept the whole law from his youth up (Mark 10:17-31; Matthew 19:16-30; Luke 18:18-30). Could that be true? No, the rich young ruler simply refused to admit his sin. To him every single thought, word, and action from his youth up was righteous. So, the Lord Jesus told him to sell all he had. If he was as righteous as he claimed (which no can be), then there was only one thing higher: sell all and follow Jesus. This he refused demonstrating his most obvious sin besides pride which was greed. So, this rich young ruler left Jesus with his self-righteousness and wealth intact but not saved. Kingdom people will always admit their sin and ask for forgiveness on a regular basis. We must stand before the Lord and tell Him the sinful thoughts, words, and actions we have committed. Then we agree with Him that they were sinful and violated His law.

The second aspect of repentance is to mourn over those sins. In the Beatitudes, the Lord Jesus speaks of the spiritual characteristics of His children. Though these qualities appear physical, they really refer to spiritual aspects of his kingdom people. In Matthew 5:3, Jesus declares, "Blessed are the poor in spirit, for theirs is the kingdom of God." There is no virtue in being poor. He was speaking of those poor in their spirit. The Greek word translated "poor" means "bankrupt" and refers to the acknowledgement that His people know they are spiritually bankrupt in sin. This is the first aspect, we just discussed. The Lord Jesus continues in verse 4, "Blessed are those who mourn, for they shall be comforted." This remark speaks of mourning over our bankrupt condition before God as one mourns over the dead. It refers to a deep sorrow over our sin and wickedness, which is the second aspect. When someone receives the Lord, they admit their sins while they mourn, grieve, and sorrow over them. In the same way, as we live our Christians lives, we will be constantly convicted of our sins and are to admit them to the Lord Jesus. Then, we will experience a sorrowful grieving process when we fully face what we did. There is sorrow and mourning over sin.

In 1 Corinthians, Paul describes the sins and difficulties this church encountered because they had been prideful and rebellious. Paul was deeply hurt because the church had taken a stand against him. False prophets had risen up and found a leader in the church. This sinful leader with most of the church stood against Paul, the apostle, and his ministry. As a result, the apostle was forced to send a difficult and confrontational letter referred to in 2 Corinthians 2:3-4. When he finally visited, they did not respond well. So, he shortened his visit and departed. Later, Paul sent Titus to discover their final response to his rebuke. When Titus returned, he brought great news of the church's repentance (2 Corinthians).

In 2 Corinthians 7:9, Paul vividly described the extent of their sorrow, grief, and mourning over their sin. He wrote, "I now rejoice, not that you were made sorry, but...you were made sorry to repentance. For you were made sorry in a godly way, that you might suffer loss by us in nothing." He spoke of their godly sorrow which produces the repentance leading to salvation. This is the sorrow Christians have when they come to Christ and every day of their lives thereafter. He contrasts this with another kind of grief in verse 10, "For godly sorrow works repentance to salvation, which brings no regret. But the sorrow of the world works death." The godly sorrow leads to salvation and the other to damnation. The ungodly sorrow leads to despair and guilt-ridden anguish.

The first is the sorrow expressed by the woman who came to Jesus in Luke 7:37-39. This grieving woman washed His feet with her many tears and wiped them with her hair in sorrow over her sin! Then, she kissed His feet and anointed them with expensive perfume. What humility and mourning over wrong-doing! The second sorrow produces bitterness, despair, anger, and pride. It desires to lash out at others for hurting them, rebuking them, or interrupting their sin. This emotion vents at oneself in punishment and self-hatred. It will not admit sin and plead for forgiveness. For this reason, we must fully deal with our sin and accept the Lord God's forgiveness.

The third aspect in repentance is the repentance of sins. Though this word is used with a fuller meaning in defining the entire concept, it also has a unique meaning of its own. The Greek word translated "repent" means "to turn around in the opposite direction or change one's mind or behavior." We must turn around from our confessed sins and move in the opposite direction. We must commit ourselves to living differently.

Luke records Peter's denial of even knowing the Lord in Luke 22:62 and how the apostle wept in sorrow and remorse afterward. Later, Luke records in Acts chapter two, three, and other passages the many sermons that Peter preached in great boldness for Christ. Peter clearly demonstrated that he had turned in the opposite direction from that sin. Of course, the Holy Spirit will provide the strength needed in order to accomplish this supernatural feat (Acts 2:4; Romans 8:13). Now, consider the response of Judas. In Matthew 27:3-9, he would not repent nor humble himself before the Lord Jesus and remove the guilt and sorrow through salvation. Instead, he simply killed himself to alleviate his anguish and torment from his betrayal. This is the sorrow unto death. We can confess our sins through three simple steps.

The first important step in the confession process is the recognition that no matter who else we have sinned against, we have sinned against our God first. Therefore, when we have sinned and desire to confess, we must initially ask God for forgiveness and reconcile with Him before we reconcile with others. It is His law that was broken. Why? It is His standards and ordinances that we are violating. Therefore, we must go before the throne and face our Father.

This is found in Psalm 51. David has just committed the sins of adultery and murder, which have been exposed. He opens the psalm crying out for God's mercy. He begs God for the forgiveness of these horrible transgressions and asks Him to wash him thoroughly from these sins and make him clean again. Then in Psalm 51:4, David utters, "Against you, and you only, have I sinned, and done that which is evil in your sight; that you may be proved right when you speak, and justified when you judge."

The word translated "only" in the English does not refer to God as the only one transgressed. Instead, it has the idea of "separate from." King David is stating that His transgression against God is completely separate, wholly different, and stands alone when compared to anyone else that has been transgressed. He had sinned against Bathsheba, Uriah, their families, and even the nation of Israel as their leader, but this cannot be compared to the gravity and the seriousness of his sin against God. Why? God is above all else in the universe (Psalm 115:3). He is the ruler of all nations (Psalm 22:28) and the sovereign God (Ephesians 1:11). God is the law giver, and His law has been transgressed (James 2:10; 4:12). Most of all, His Son is our Lord (Romans 10:12-13). He was present listening to the conversation as we argued. He stands before us in every transgression. He must be asked for forgiveness. The ones who have been transgressed do not set standards of behavior; God alone does. He must be faced first.

The Lord God must be dealt with on a separate and utterly divine level before all others in the transgression. In Psalm 41:4, David again takes up the lament of his wickedness, which brought reprisal from his enemies. The king cries, "I said, 'Yahweh, have mercy on me! Heal me, for I have sinned against you.'" Then this great king paints a beautiful picture of the relief he experiences in forgiveness. In Psalm 41:11-13, he shouts this, "By this I know that you delight in me, because my enemy doesn't triumph over me. As for me, you uphold me in my integrity...set me in your presence forever. Blessed be Yahweh...from everlasting and to everlasting! Amen and amen."

Luke describes Saul as "ravaging" the church. He went from house to house dragging off Christian men and women and had them thrown in prison. As the saints were scattered because of the persecution, Saul followed them breathing threats and murder against them. As the apostle wrote to young Timothy, a trusted companion and fellow pastor, he remembered the horrific affliction he had brought upon those innocent Christians and the mercy he received in God's forgiveness. In 1 Timothy 1, Paul characterizes himself as a violent blasphemer, persecutor, aggressor, and the foremost of all sinners. Then in verses 14-15, the apostle describes the open arms of God in forgiveness as he came in repentance. Paul writes, "The grace of our Lord abounded exceedingly with faith and love which is in Christ Jesus. The saying is faithful and worthy of all acceptance that Christ Jesus came into the world to save sinners; of whom I am chief." The Lord Jesus Christ came into the world to die so God could open His loving and powerful arms toward us in His marvelous and abundant grace!

Paul continues to marvel at the grace, love, and mercy he experienced as he came before the Lord in repentance. No matter how heinous the transgression is, how disgusting is the sin, or even how atrocious is the iniquity, when we come before almighty God, His arms are outstretched, his hands are open, and His heart is ready to forgive. His grace, mercy, and love will outpour into forgiveness when we come to confess our sins. Our God is a Father who is always ready to forgive.

When we sin against God, He never forsakes us. Instead, God waits in readiness for our return to Him in repentance and confession. David acknowledges this in his Psalm 86:5, when the king wrote, "For you, Lord, are good, and ready to forgive; abundant in loving kindness to all those who call on you." This God of ours is ready to forgive when we sin. He is full of love and kindness to all who call upon Him. Then in verse 8, he shouts, "There is no one like you among the gods, Lord, nor any deeds like your deeds." In the midst of God's willingness to forgive, He only demands that we come to Him first to reconcile our relationships. He is our Lord; we must humble ourselves before His presence in repentance, before we humble ourselves before others.

Next, we should not leave anything out. As we walk into God's presence to ask for forgiveness, we must realize God knows the entire story and every detail of what we have done. As we confess our transgressions, we must admit to all of them holding nothing back. There may be times, where it would be too hurtful and not edifying to disclose everything, we thought or may have said in private to the people we have wronged, but we should confess these to God. We will take the true responsibility we had for what happened. Then, we should go to the others that have been wronged and ask for forgiveness.

Confession before God involves the acknowledgement of all our sin. In Psalm 32:3-4, David describes the torment he felt when he refused to confess all his sins and kept them bottled up inside. He sobs, "When I kept silence, my bones wasted away through my groaning all day long. For day and night your hand was heavy on me. My strength was sapped in the heat of summer. Selah." Then in the next verse, he finally acknowledges all his sin. In Psalm 32:5, he continues, "I acknowledged my sin to you. I didn't hide my iniquity. I said, I will confess my transgressions to Yahweh, and you forgave the iniquity of my sin. Selah." Then King David describes the incredible relief and release he experiences. In Psalm 32:11, he adds, "Be glad in Yahweh, and rejoice, you righteous! Shout for joy, all you who are upright in heart!" We can experience His relief.

In Psalm 90:8, Moses acknowledges this when he asserts, "You have set our iniquities before you, our secret sins in the light of your presence." Both Moses and the nation of Israel had a problem with sin, and he states that their iniquities and sin were before the Lord, even the hidden ones. These secret transgressions that no one knows about are exposed in the light of God's Holy presence. The light of God's holiness exposes all our sins, even the ones no one else knows about. Moses is explaining that the Lord sees every sin. We cannot hide any iniquity from Him. Once we become cognizant of His presence, His light exposes our sin.

Since God can look deeply into the recesses of our hearts and minds, He can also clearly see our motives and reasons for our behavior toward others. In Proverbs 17:3, Solomon adds, "The refining pot is for silver, and the furnace for gold, but Yahweh tests the hearts." In Proverbs 16:2, the wise king declared, "All the ways of a man are clean in his own eyes; but Yahweh weighs the motives." As God is weighing our hearts, we may see some thought, word, or action as of no account or even righteous, but God may judge it differently. He may see it as evil. So, we must go before God with every thought, word, and action in our hearts and minds and lay them bare before Him. How do we do this?

Through prayer, we ask the Holy Spirit to convict us of any transgression in the breakup of the relationship that we have committed. One of the responsibilities of the Holy Spirit in our lives is to convict us of sin (John 16:8). How does our God do this? In Psalm 139:23-24, David beseeches, "Search me, God, and know my heart. Try me and know my thoughts." Then he adds, "See if there is any wicked way in me, and lead me in the everlasting way." He searches our hearts and reveals them to us.

Third, we must accept God's forgiveness. When we sin, our relationship with the Lord God has been damaged, and God must be dealt with first. To restore our relationship with Him, we are to lay out our sins before Him and take full responsibility for them. We are to admit that they are wrong and ask Him for forgiveness. So, the next step is to accept our God's forgiveness with a sense of blessing and gratefulness. Since this is a deeply spiritual process, there may not be a great feeling of relief. When this occurs, we should claim His forgiveness by faith in Him. After David sinned against God by taking Bathsheba and murdering her husband, the king wrote psalm 51.

In this psalm he has this relational forgiveness in mind. In verse 8, he writes in joy, "Let me hear joy and gladness, that the bones which you have broken may rejoice." Then in verse 10, he continues, "Create in me a clean heart, O God. Renew a right spirit within me." In verse 12, he entreats, "Restore to me the joy of your salvation. Uphold me with a willing spirit." Then in verse 14-15, he says, "Deliver me from the guilt of bloodshed [sin], O God, the God of my salvation. My tongue shall sing aloud of your righteousness. Lord, open my lips. My mouth shall declare your praise."

How can we feel real relief from the burden of our evil, as we confess our sins to the Lord God? We claim it by faith as

David did. He knew His God had forgiven Him. In fact, the prophet Nathan had confirmed this very fact when he was confronted by him. In 2 Samuel 12:13, when David declared that he had sinned, Nathan responded, "Yahweh also has put away your sin." Though David knew he was forgiven from a salvation point of view, he needed his relationship with God fully restored and deeply desired the relief, sense of blessing, and thankfulness that pours out of an authentic confession. We find relief and joy that comes when we have fully admitted our sin, mourned over it, and turned from it.

While confessing our sins, we should continually remind ourselves of Christ's removal of all our debts. In Colossians 2:13-14, the apostle describes this momentous event, "You were dead in your trespasses and the uncircumcision of your flesh. He made you alive together with him, having forgiven us all our trespasses, wiping out the certificate of debt which was decrees against us; and he has taken it out of the way, nailing it to the cross" (DEJ). Christ has taken the certificate of debt consisting of decrees against us and has nailed them to the cross. Every decree of judgment against us for every sin we ever commit, are committing, or will ever commit has been nailed to the cross and we can accept this by faith. This brings a sense of blessing and gratitude producing relief.

In Revelation 1:5, John opens the last book of the Bible in these words, "And from Jesus Christ, the faithful witness, the firstborn of the dead, and the ruler of the kings of the earth. To him who loves us, and washed us from our sins by his blood." When we received Jesus Christ, we were washed in His blood eternally; when we confess our sins, forgiveness keeps flowing relationally. This is a powerful truth. Our sins are washed away. They are gone.

As we confess our sins after our salvation, our fellowship with the Lord is continually restored. In Psalm 28:7, King David testifies of his thanksgiving, joy, and blessing to the Lord God, "Yahweh is my strength and my shield. My heart has trusted in him, and I am helped. Therefore, my heart greatly rejoices. With my song I will thank him." Then, in verse 8, he continues, "Yahweh is their strength. He is a stronghold of salvation to his anointed." What an amazing and incredible sense of blessing and thanksgiving pouring forth in praise of God! Once we have involved God first, left nothing out in our confession, we accept His forgiveness for what we have done.

Now, we have learned that living the Christian life will involve confession and forgiveness. To find true release for our captive hearts from fear, pain, emptiness, regret, tragedy, guilt, despair, brokenness, anxiety, aimlessness, and much uncertainty, we include stumbling and falling along the way. The old habits of coping are hard to give up. We will face the temptation to develop new sinful approaches to handling the chains rather than holy ones. No matter how much we desire not to sin, we still will. As a result, we must be prepared to stumble, fall, confess, and begin the walk again. This may occur many times a day at first but as we grow in Christ it decreases. As our holy lives increase, we should experience more and more calm, peace, joy, faith, comfort, hope, love, grace, courage, purpose, and trust.

Conclusion

Paul had been mobbed by the Jews as he was fulfilling a holy vow in the temple. Though the apostle was attempting to demonstrate his devotion to the Jewish people, instead they accused him of bringing a Gentile into the sacred area. A Roman centurion intervened, and Paul was arrested. This began four years of house arrest while the governors tried to decide what to do with him. When it looked as if he would be sent back for a trial before the Jewish Council, the apostle exercised his Roman right to appeal to Caesar.

After his nephew disclosed a plot by a band of Jews to ambush and kill Paul, the centurion sent him to Rome with a regiment of soldiers guarding him. After boarding a vessel headed for Rome, the apostle barely survived a shipwreck at sea. When Paul arrived in the capital city, he was shackled to an imperial guard night and day while he awaited his trial before the emperor. Though Paul should have experienced the chains of emptiness, fear of death, physical pain, stress, desperation, despair, regret, guilt, brokenness, uncertainty, or worry, he felt free amid this difficult moment.

How is this possible? No matter what circumstances Paul encountered, he was always growing in his Christian life by walking with spiritual intention, consistently studying the Scriptures, persisting in watchful prayer, seeking personal holiness, fellowshipping with steady interaction, sharing the gospel, utilizing his spiritual gifts in ministry, expecting and winning the spiritual battles against the forces of darkness, and humbly confessing when he did not. This brought Paul calm, peace, joy, faith, comfort, hope, love, purpose, courage, grace, purpose, and trust. He was learning how to measure up to the stature of Christ. He was handling the issues he faced in his imprisonment as Christ had his journey to the

FREE AMID LIFE'S DIFFICULT MOMENTS

cross. The Holy Spirit provided His fruits as he yielded to Him. As the apostle was able to find freedom through the principles of spiritual growth so can we.

As we peer into the letters He wrote during this time, we see these principles in action. In Philippians 3:17, the apostle Paul exhorted, "Brothers, be imitators together of me, and note those who walk this way, even as you have us for an example." He was walking intentionally in his growth and wanted the church to do the same. In Colossians 1:25-26, Paul wrote these words, "Of which I was made a servant, according to the stewardship of God which was given me toward you, to fulfill the word of God, the mystery which has been hidden for ages and generations. But now it has been revealed to his saints." The apostle Paul saw himself as having a stewardship given to him to fulfill the Word and to proclaim the mystery of Christ. He accomplished this study and preaching of the Word of God in his many writings and sermons during this difficult time.

While in prison he persisted in watchful prayer. He told the church in Ephesus that he was always praying for them. In Ephesians 1:16, he described his prayers, "Don't cease to give thanks for you, making mention of you in my prayers." In his physical chains, he was still living a righteous life in such a way that he was able to tell them to imitate him. In Philippians 4:9, he commanded them to resist anxiety and take all their concerns to prayer. While doing this, they were to follow his righteous lifestyle. He pens, "The things which you learned, received, heard, and saw in me: do these things, and the God of peace will be with you." We know Paul was sharing the gospel because he told the church in Philippi that many of the guards and Caesar's household had come to Christ (Philippians 1:13; 4:22). In fact, Paul's courage had made the Roman saints bolder to share the gospel in the city themselves (Philippians 1:14).

Since he was allowed to have visitors, he was able to have a steady interaction with the saints. Notice his statement at the end of Philippians. In chapter 4:21-22, he concludes, "Greet every saint in Christ Jesus. The brothers who are with me greet you. All the saints greet you, especially those who are of Caesar's household." In Romans 7:19, Paul describes his deep struggle with sin, "'For the good which I desire, I don't do; but the evil which I don't desire, that I practice." Since humble confession is a part of every believer's life, we know Paul dealt with his sin the same way. So, we now know how to deal with the captivity we feel through growth in Christ spiritually and supernaturally.

I would like to conclude with this admonition: Live the Christian life to the fullest and let the Spirit work. If you still have not been able to find and unshackle your chains, then read my final book in this series. The third book will address the issues that still remain.

One Last Thought:

As a Christian Pastoral Counselor addressing very serious life problems in this book, I recognize the possibility that someone might be reading this and contemplating suicide. If this is the case, please do not hesitate to call 911 or go to the nearest emergency room or hospital immediately.

(And take this book with you!)

ABOUT THE AUTHOR

Dr. Donald Jones is currently a Christian Pastoral Counselor with thirty-eight years of experience in the fields of pastoral ministry, public education, and Christian counseling. He carries degrees and certificates from four major universities and from a variety of educational institutions. He has been a professor of Languages and Bible, a television commentator, and a featured speaker at a variety of events and seminars at churches, schools, and other organizations across the United States. He is a member in good standing of several secular and Christian professional organizations. Dr. Jones has been a published author since 1976. For further information view his website at www.donjonesphd.com.